SmartZen

How to adopt the Zen approach to life and business for a wealthier, healthier and happier life with a touch of Japanese wisdom.

Yumi Merricks

Published in Great Britain 2019

By Billie Vinue Ltd.

Cover Design ©Billie Vinue Ltd.

Editing by: Leina Mancuso

ISBN: 978-1-5272-5547-0

DEDICATION

I dedicate this book to people who are on their own path
toward light and awakening.

CONTENTS

"If you are unable to find the truth right where
you are, where else do you expect to find it?"
— *Dogen*

INTRODUCTION

If you have been working hard to succeed but have not got there yet, this book explains some of the reasons why and what you can do to change it.

If you are feeling some kind of resistance, obstacles or challenges that are stopping you from earning more money, being happier and feeling healthier, this book is going to teach you how to overcome them easily and effortlessly.

The society is waking up.

Even though most of us grew up believing; success will bring us happiness and fulfilment, the reality is that most of us are feeling stressed and unfulfilled.

People generally work hard in order to increase their annual income, but as numerous studies have shown, even when the annual income reaches over a certain level, happiness level does not necessarily grow in a linear way in proportion to the increase in income.

On the other hand, people who are already happy are living longer, having better overall health and being more productive in their profession and in their business, and as a result, leading a fulfilled life not necessarily having a direct correlation to the level of income or wealth.

Many people have already woken up to the reality that happiness is the key to success.

But sustaining that happiness is not always easy in today's world.

This book will show you how you can transform your life from being stuck, stressed and unfulfilled to resurrecting and reaching your dream, being your authentic self and creating an abundant life full of passion and purpose for the rest of your life.

This book is based on the following fundamental scientific truth.

'Everything in the universe is made up of atoms'.

Your body, other people's body, your pets and even the chair you are sitting on are made of the same stuff. Some stuff seems to be solid, but this is because of a reaction of the electrons to your touch.

But this is not a book of science.

This book is also based on ancient Japanese Zen philosophy.

Energy is all around us and within us.

You don't have to understand how it works.

You can learn to direct energy to bring health, wealth and happiness to you and to others.

This teaching can be applied across every field from personal setting to business.

But this is not a book of philosophy.

This book brings science and philosophy together and solves the most pressing topic of humankind;

How to live a happy, healthy and abundant life without destroying our planet or increasing the division between the poor and the rich.

This book will help you grow your business and career with a clear conscience and to show you, you are here on earth to fulfil your potential and to create something much bigger than wealth for you and your family.

HOW YOU WORK

"It all depends on you. You can go on sleeping forever, or you can wake up right this moment. "
– Osho

We all want success and happiness

We all work hard to get both happiness and success.

We want to be happy, and we believe it will come as a result of our actions. We pursue success. Success in our careers, success in relationships, and success in business.

Most people who start their own business, pursue a high-end freelancing career or become an entrepreneur dream of the time when they eventually achieve success and imagine their lives to be easier, fulfilled with freedom and happiness.

An entrepreneur's journey is not an easy ride. Success does not happen overnight. Many hours may have to be invested into the business before you can see the fruits of your labour. But you carry on believing that one day, very soon, that your business will thrive, and all the stress will be over.

Meanwhile, you lock yourself away from your family, stop socialising with your friends and postpone pursuing your hobby. Even people who don't run their own business and work for an employer, they are generally so stressed most of the time, they are unable to switch off from work.

Because you have learned to measure your success by the productivity and how close you get to your goals. Because you have grown to believe that happiness will be a natural result of attaining that success.

But…

Scientific research shows that it is not the success that brings happiness and good health; it is the other way around.

What research has found is that people who are happy become successful and perceive themselves as more successful than people who are financially affluent but unhappy.

If you have been putting the maintenance of your health, mental wellbeing and even your relationship with loved ones on hold until you achieve success, because you believe you will come to a point in which you will be totally happy, you may end up delaying living a happy life for years. Meanwhile, you might burn yourself out with stress.

The reality of delaying happiness and fulfilment until the arrival of success is that when success finally happens if, at all, it can come at the expense of health or relationships.

You may find yourself disconnected with the loved ones to enjoy the success with. You may find you have risked your health and well-being and are now not able to enjoy your life in the way you had imagined.

Then you wonder what all those years you struggled were for. You didn't want your life to be left behind. Was this exactly the reason you got away from the rat race and started your own journey as an entrepreneur?

We are programmed to believe that sacrifice brings success. We learned to delay gratification from an early age. We were disciplined to wait for the good stuff, like earning more money, receiving recognition or attaining a 'success' in our field.

I don't believe that just sitting around wishing for success to arrive without taking any actions will brings success. Delaying gratification is an important skill you learn as a child that helps achieve success as an adult.

As a life coach, it is our job to help clients set goals and take actions towards achieving them.

However, just constantly focusing on taking actions with future goals in mind does not necessarily make you more productive or help success to happen more quickly. You may temporarily feel a sense of achievement when certain milestones are achieved, but you may not have recognised it as happiness in its own right.

We need to see a bigger picture of how success and happiness are related to each other.

It is true that a lack of money and resources affects the level of happiness in people. Those who are in financial difficulty are in general, more stressed and unhappy.

But there is scientific proof that financial success mainly comes as a result of being happy, contrary to a belief that success is a source of happiness.

Should you stop pursuing success?

No.

It is in our nature to grow and reach our full potential.

Success does not guarantee happiness nor does being rich. But this does not mean you must stop pursuing success.

Because it is not either-or.

It is possible to have both.

You just need to find happiness first before success.

This also applies to success in a romantic relationship. Be happy first and you will find love.

It sounds like a paradox but it's not an unsolvable one.

If you switch your way of thinking and start believing that you need to find happiness and fulfilment first, your success will follow.

How do you find happiness and well-being first when you are not yet successful?

That is where the ancient Japanese Zen wisdom comes in. The word, 'Zen' has now become widely used in the English language. In the West, people interpret its meaning as something along the lines of letting go of what cannot be controlled.

Perhaps your image of Zen is of a Buddhist monk sitting in

front of a Zen garden meditating.

While these are elements of Zen philosophy, it may not yet be clear to you how this can apply to you or relate to your success in business and personal life.

Living SmartZen is not living your life with sacrifice. It does not mean you must be passive or you should allow other people to walk all over you.

SmartZen is not about compromising your dreams and aspirations.

SmartZen is in no way a lenient approach to life.

SmartZen is to have clarity, vision and inner strength.

SmartZen is about living in the present and fulfilling your potential.

SmartZen is leading a harmonious life that is better for all.

In this book, you will learn that Zen is not only about meditating in silence or not reacting to life's struggles. It will teach you that you are a part of a large network and how that translates into the daily life that leads to you attaining your goals in life.

By understanding the simple fundamentals of viewing your body, mind and soul as parts of a larger interconnected network rather than separate things you need to work on individually, you will begin to learn how to bring harmony and balance into your life. You will know that achieving happiness is naturally followed by success.

This does not mean you need to lock yourself in a monastery for weeks or go on a strict detox.

Trying for a sudden transformation like that rarely gives you a lasting change in your well-being.

A couple of weeks later you will be back to square one because that experience was too far-fetched from the reality of your everyday life.

It's a bit like, at the end of a wonderful vacation, some of us mutter that the holiday is over, and we have to get back to 'reality'.

But when you learn the way of SmartZen there will be no need to feel this distinction anymore.

Happiness and success will be a reality.

You may have already adopted part of the Eastern philosophy and are practising meditation.

That is good.

But meditating every morning and night while for the rest of the waking hours you abuse your body in some ways by over-eating, drinking and depriving of sleep, mixing with a wrong crowd, meditation alone cannot contribute enough to your well-being as a whole.

It sounds like common sense but adopting bits of wisdom here and there and liking motivational and Zen quotes on Instagram might make you feel less guilty about your other abusive behaviour, but it won't work as a long-term solution.

SmartZen can be adopted to your daily life in bringing daily harmony. Learning new ways to think and do will become a habit that will bring about a lasting effect on your well-being. Your happiness and fulfilment go hand in hand with your well-being and success in business and in life will follow.

Because when you are happy, you will naturally attract more positive events, positive people and positive energy to your life.

You may have to read this book more than once. But in doing so, the idea of living with total harmony will become a norm and a habit for you. You will realise that you had all the ingredients to success and happiness within yourself all along.

You just needed to learn how to unlock them and put them all together in an effective way and make it work for you.

Once you are leading this state of being, you will be surprised how fast your success starts happening.

Throughout the book, I will mention the frequency of vibration, the flow of energy, feeling oneness, universal intelligence and being in harmony, many times. I would like you to know that I am talking about the same thing. You can call this whatever you like and have your own words to describe it.

But the key ingredient for the transformation is maintaining the state when you feel the harmony or realignment that I talk about within yourself. As you read, you will experience the distinct flow of energy simultaneously.

When you get it, you will know this physiologically instantly what I am talking about as if a last piece of the puzzle just found its place in the 32 trillion pieces of particles in your body.

As you read, start implementing the idea straight away, not later when you have finished the book. You will get better value out of this book and start to see and feel that your life begins to transform.

I really hope you love reading this book. I would love to know how you got on. Do let me know by contacting me on our website.

Why Do You Need To Work So Hard?

Most of us live in a world where most of our basic needs had been met a long ago. We have shelter, food and clothing and much more. A world where there is more stuff than we could ever use them. Yet we continue to drown ourselves in the mountains of material goods.

Don't get me wrong, I do like having material things including useful gadgets and beautiful objects. I also admit sometimes I make an irrational decision on my purchases.

But if you are shopping in compensation to how stressed you feel inside or you are buying 'stuff' to aid your emotional needs for temporary happiness, it is time to review your habits.

This includes shopping for things you don't actually need. Things that you buy on a whim and spending money as soon as you earn some because you somehow 'believe' in your mind you need it and you deserve it. You believe buying this item is an act of self-love because you are convinced you should not deprive yourself of this self-love.

This might also be because you feel some kind of pressure to keep up with the Jones' or to prove to others, and perhaps to yourself, that you are doing quite well. You may have not noticed doing this on a conscious level or you have never connected the two in the past.

Your brain can create superficial happiness and perceived success. Some people measure the level of success with the market price for their material possessions rather than the value of their net assets including the level of happiness. They cannot stop this vicious circle of material gathering, just in order to keep feeling the 'high'.

Consumerism is addictive and can be an abuse on our well-being like any other addiction.

Others spend their money because they need to reward themselves with something so that they can keep coping with the pressure of work, family and other demands in life.

And we continue to spend what we earn on more things we don't need as if, they will bring us lasting joy.

But do they?

In 2015, a survey commissioned by Virgin[1] stated that '51% of full-time UK employees said they have experienced anxiety or 'burnout' in their current job'. In another study the same year, almost half (45 per cent) of employees said they didn't have enough time each week to do personal activities.[2]

Three years on in 2018, how did this change?

526,000 workers in the UK suffered from work-related stress, depression or anxiety in 2016 to 17 according to

Health and Safety Executive research published in 2018.[*3]

Scientists tell us that our brain has not caught up with the speed in which our lives changed over the last few decades. The industrial revolution and the advancement in technology have transformed our lives beyond recognition from the times that our lives were simpler, slow-paced, and more locally based.

Instead, people are now living and working in an environment where competition is fierce both at work and in social life. We often travel long distances just to get to work each day. Having to be continually productive and proving our worth both to our boss and to ourselves has made our brain stay in the constant state of 'fight or flight' mode, which is the brain's defence mechanism for dangerous situations. Like the caveman fighting the tiger!

What seems to have happened is that people who are in this state day after day have exhausted themselves, burned out, stressed and or depressed.

It is worrying that it has become a trend to show off the length of your 'to-do list' or how much pressure you are under as if it is a proof of your success or a badge of honour you wear with pride.

So, we are still struggling.

We continue to struggle to balance work and life and to find happiness.

We struggle to see that beauty of our life lies within us and we take this for granted as if this body and soul are here to last infinitely. We focus on achievements and the next goal when what we strive to get is already here.

It is time we get the balance right.

A phrase like work-life balance did not get used so much in our parents' generation.

Japan is one of the countries with the longest working hours per week on average. The origin of the word 'Karoshi'; death by overworking is Japan.

Some employers in the West have begun to take this seriously and have realised that simply providing them with a private medical service package as an employee benefit no longer counts as helpful or attractive enough to retain good talent.

Those employers are waking up to the fact that giving an intangible benefit of helping employees find a better work-life balance is what is needed to keep the good staff from leaving them.

As we understand the relationship between our mind and body, we know that stress hormones produced during chronic stress or constant pressure actually damage us physiologically, too.

Physiological symptoms manifest themselves in many different ways such as pain or swelling, leading to weakening of our immune system and permanent damages to cells, eventually causing physical diseases. Sometimes such diseases are incurable and affecting our well-being in many ways.

There is a Japanese proverb, 'yamai wa ki kara', which translates 'illness comes from the state of one's mind'. When your mind is healthy, your body will sync and, you will experience optimal health.

Let's talk about how you can change your life from being stressful to getting your balance back.

The fact is most people spend 8-10 hours a day working.

That is 60%-80% of waking hours on weekdays. That is why most people have to cram every other activity at weekends and end up having no time to de-stress, relax or rejuvenate in preparation for the new working week.

As I said earlier, some people are so stressed that they feel the need to treat themselves with something, instant gratification of some sort in compensation for their hard work and stress. It could be a new car, a new handbag or a new gadget for instant joy and superficial happiness.

Some parents teach the same to their children, too. Exhausted, parents choose to buy their children another toy, instead of spending quality time together. It is often the easiest option for working parents and to relieve themselves of that guilt of not being around for them. These children might also grow up to rely on material items to fulfil their needs. So, the cycle continues.

I cannot stress enough how important it is for you to enjoy what you do for work. Whether this is for earning money or activities you do to build your business. Because you spend many hours each day doing this, it needs to be an activity that you in your heart truly feels 'right'. When it does, it should bring out the best version of yourself.

Recently the word, 'passion' is mentioned a lot in the

business world. People are encouraged to do what they are passionate about. But passion alone is not enough to gauge how much your work is aligned with who you truly are.

You may need to dig deeper. This might mean questioning not only your job role and what you do to earn money but also who you work with and the organisation or the network you belong to.

Are you satisfied with what you do for work and the future prospects of the work despite some ups and downs that is to be expected?

Do you connect well with people you work with? Is working with them uplifting and replenishes good energy for all concerned?

Do you agree with how your company or organisation treat their people and do you believe how the business operates is in line with your ethical standards to humans and the planet?

If you are not able to answer yes to most of the questions above, what the heck are you doing allowing yourself to be in such toxic environment day after day?

Throughout my time working as an employee, whatever company I worked for there were colleagues muttering time and time again something like, 'the money's good but the job is s***' or 'I am so unhappy and I want to quit but I can't leave because I will not find another job that pays as well as this one'.

So, they stay and put up with it for a few more years and in some cases until retirement because they 'believe' they do not have a choice. They tend to think that there is some kind of an external force preventing them from moving on or has placed them in this predicament without hope. Most of the time, I noticed these people were not only unhappy but also suffered from some kind of physical illness or disorder.

If you are someone who has always worked for yourself, you probably don't understand what it is like to be trapped in this sort of situation. But for those who have only been an employee are often unaware of their own power to change their situation, usually until something drastic happens and they are forced to make a change.

Maybe you are a self-employed person who has learned skills and trade or have a client base you are afraid to leave behind because of that security you feel which as a result, is preventing you from taking your life in a new direction.

Maybe as a fresh university graduate who accepted any job that was available because you are tied to a debt you must payback.

This seemingly serious inability to change their situation usually stems from a fear of unknown and or lack of confidence in themselves. Sure, it is sometimes scary to leave your job and start your own business or change your job to a slightly lower-paid one which might be what you really want to do to ignite your passion for work. Because you don't know whether you can afford to live without the level of financial comfort you got used to, the decision seems hard.

However, you might find it surprising how little you actually need to meet your basic needs though.

Regardless of what salary you perceive necessary as a minimum, if you are choosing the salary, benefits, convenience, status or even the company brand of your current job over your personal well-being, you will find yourself to be always 'stuck'.

But when you start to choose what you do for work, based on your own value and life's purpose, you will enjoy inner peace, total balance and fulfilment and joy. You will realise that there was no need to fear and you should have made this transition much earlier.

Because you will find a way to make the transition work as you develop trust in yourself, and success and happiness will arrive. As you go through this book, you will learn how to develop this trust and confidence to transform your life for the better.

26

WHAT IS SMARTZEN?

"Think with your whole body."

-Taisen Deshimaru

What an ancient Zen philosophy got to do with our lives in the 21st Century anyway?

Okay, okay.

The benefits of living in the present and attaining that calm through meditation is not a new idea.

In fact, meditation has become so popular that nowadays everyone seems to be doing this.

Some research showed that 8% of all Americans said they mediated regularly.

Even at the World Economic Forum in Davos in 2018, morning meditation sessions were held for the attendees.

Sitting in silence for a few minutes once or twice a day helps calm the mind and your energy re-centred. The benefit of refocusing your breath and bringing your attention back to the present can become a habit that develops through practice.

Some forward-thinking employers and organisations are providing space or a quiet room for their staff to do this during the working day. This is such good news as the meditation has become something that is no longer a foreign idea, just like the idea of eating raw fish.

I remember when I first came to live in the UK in the early 1980s, most people who had not tried sushi were revolted at the thought of eating fish uncooked. In those days, in the kitchens of English families, I saw that fish were boiled, well, to death, until all the nutrients and taste disappeared from it. 'That is a terrible waste', I thought.

Back then, Japanese food shops and restaurants in London were there to cater mainly for the Japanese expatriates and their families who were seconded to their company's UK office for a duration of a few years. The only type of takeaways you could buy from high streets were hamburgers, Chinese meals and fish and chips.

How far have we come?

Over the last 35 years or so, how the Western people have embraced Japanese cuisine is something I did not imagine at the time.

The increase in the popularity of Japanese food is evident.

However, there is more to the Japanese food and culture

than enjoying sushi being delivered on a conveyor belt.

Likewise, there is more to meditation than closing your eyes for a few minutes each day.

For many years I had found it hard to integrate or explain the particular 'state of being' in a way that could be blended into the Western tradition. Moreover, in the past, I could not imagine this state of being to be any use in business or in the corporate world.

The fundamental belief of how we view our body, mind and soul as a whole had been strange for the masses in the West until quite recently.

When I found a similar belief in the West over thirty years ago, it was regarded as esoteric or occult. As soon as I started mentioning the flow of energy, the frequency of vibration, the universe or 'oneness', I was at the risk of being branded a hippy, talking some kind of mysticism or magic.

Others might have thought I was bonkers.

People who spoke of these universal powers and used for

good in the past were treated like witches. Other people termed it 'wishy-washy'.

The idea that the energy, body and mind are connected to and intermingled with each other got regarded as another type of religious belief rather than a way of life.

I felt back then that it was not accepted by the norm or a part of everyday life. Given the history of how people with these beliefs were treated in the West, (some allegedly burned on the stake), it is understandable the knowledge remained hidden from the Western public for many years.

This lack of understanding also translated into how we viewed our body and how illnesses were treated. In most cases, I found that the treatment in the West was based on relieving the symptoms rather than treating the cause. This was because Western medicine used to view our body as a machine made up of different components.

In the 1980s, complementary therapies such as homoeopathy and acupuncture were considered as an 'alternative'. It was not until after the millennium that the UK's National Health Service began providing natural therapies like these as part of their medical service and called it 'complimentary' to Western medicine.

Psychology and the understanding of how mind works were in no way as nearly recognised in mass thirty years ago as it is today. When people talked about mental illness, it was usually to do with patients locked up in mental hospitals. In those days, it was not considered as something we experienced in ourselves, schools or in the community around us.

The treatment of illness by viewing the whole person as one was not new in the East. We were used to thinking that the digestive system can react to anxiety and nervousness. We had an understanding that there was a connection between one part of the body with another as well as with our mind.

As a new resident of the United Kingdom, this clash of the Eastern philosophy and the Western medical science manifested itself in my mind as a major confusion. I was literally puzzled with conflicting ideas.

Back then, wanting to trust doctors and wanting to be a reasonably behaved citizen, I often tried to practice, 'when in Rome, do as the Romans do' and went with the flow.

This was until Fritjof Capra untangled this confusion for me in 1986 in a BBC documentary and his book, 'Tao of Physics'. He explained how harmony existed between the Eastern mysticism and modern quantum physics.

He explained how one afternoon sitting by the ocean, he had a direct experience with nature itself which was what he had been studying as a physicist. He knew that everything was made of vibrating particles and atoms and he experienced this within his own body as he sat on a beach.

So, there is a place where the West and the East can meet.

We know from the study of physics that everything in our body is made of the same stuff when you break it down. Our body is made up of atoms of hydrogen, carbon, nitrogen and oxygen and in between, is the energy.

But hard stuff like trees and rocks and other animals are also made up of the same fundamental pieces of the matter which are atoms.

So basically, we are all the same.

I remember the enormous relief I felt and was glad someone was able to explain it.

You might think this mind-boggling stuff only belong to the physics students learning in school but there is a huge clue we must not ignore. So, stay with me on this.

By understanding this structure and how not only our body but everything else is part of the same matter it is also part of everything that makes up our environment in the universe. We are all connected, interconnected and part of one huge network.

Sometimes you can see the evidence of this interconnectedness in nature visually when you see the murmuring flight of starling in the sky when the whole flock of birds fly together as if they are one.

Or you might have experienced when you were just thinking of someone and in the next minute, you receive a call or a text from the same person or bumped into them in town and regarded it as a 'coincidence'.

Perhaps, one time or another you felt an inclination or a strong gut feeling which you followed, and you were glad you listened to your 'instinct'.

These are evidence of a harmonious connection, synchronicity and operating in high frequency with universal intelligence.

This is the very clue for curing diseases, resolving conflicts in relationships, working as a team in organisations, ending unrest in society, and saving our beautiful planet.

When you understand this, you will begin to understand how your mind and body are interconnected. And when you understand this that you will also understand the interconnectedness with the next person and everyone else. You are also connected to the nature that surrounds you and everything else including the universe itself.

Once you know this, you will become consciously aware on a daily basis **how you work**, **how you live**, **how you relate**, **how you impact** and **how you give** affect yourself as well as others. And therefore, this understanding will affect the decisions you make on a daily basis, at work, at home and in your community.

"Everything is in the interconnected network if you are violent to part of the network, ultimately you are violent to yourself." *- Fritjof Capra*

Meditation is a process to reach this understanding within your body and mind. In the East, this is one of the ways you experience a deep spiritual awakening. This experience is not an understanding through the intellect but through direct experience within your molecules and atoms with the universal energy.

In Zen, for example, we call this basic mental state of being as 'mushin' which translates as 'no heart' or 'empty mind'. In the west, this term is used mainly in martial art disciplines such as Judo and Aikido. But the state in which we aim to reach is essentially the same.

When we are none, we are also a whole.

Taoism, Yoga and Zen all aim for the same thing, just explained slightly differently. Basically, meditation is only one of many ways to experience this spiritual awakening or enlightenment.

But in the same way no matter how many hours of meditation you do regularly, if your body, mind and soul are working separately you will never reach the harmony that the very practice of meditation teaches.

If you meditate for half an hour twice a day but you abuse or detach yourself from your body and mind for the rest of 23 hours, the shift in the consciousness will not happen through this.

For example, the number of hours you practice something is not as fruitful as when your body and mind are in complete harmony. An awoken artist, athlete or a musician will attest to this state. They might call this a flow of inspiration, or optimum performance, being in the zone or a piece of music in complete harmony. But we are talking about the same thing and we have experienced this at one time or another and we want to experience this more often.

When we connect, synchronise and adjust our frequencies to universal energy, this is when it happens. When we learn to do this every day, we raise our vibrational frequencies to tune into the abundance of the universe.

So, when we flow with universal energy, we bring inner peace and fulfilment to ourselves. As a consequence, we bring success and happiness.

For this, we can develop a profound awareness that we need to constantly strive for harmony and cooperation with the nature of our body as well as the nature that surround us instead of trying to control it.

The law of attraction theory is among those that send similar messages and there has been a significant shift in how the majority see the world and the 'nature of being' over the last few decades. A change in thinking has been happening in the last thirty years.

We now recognise the importance of being aware of how our emotions play a major part in success in academics, in business and leadership since the term 'EQ' or 'emotional intelligence' were popularised by the book of the same title in the 1990s.

It has become normal to talk about spirituality without talking about any particular religion.

Anyone and everyone are practising meditation, it's no longer distinguished as an alternative, it's become mainstream. That's such great news. Even business leaders openly mention the law of attraction or how your thoughts can manifest your desires. We are evolving as humans.

Self-awareness and meditation together with healthy eating of some Japanese food are growing in popularity, and we have finally begun to appreciate the real effects of 'the way'.

But we have further work to do to integrate a practical way of living with the very essence of Zen and to adapt this to the 21st-century living.

We are beginning to get the clarity and it is time we use some practical solutions.

SmartZen is the new Zen and it will help you get the rhythm of nature back to your life.

This idea of 'being in harmony', 'in tune with the self' or any other expression you want to call it is probably one of the hardest things to describe if you have not yet experienced this. I used to call this 'oneness with the universe' but this still does not explain it well.

You simply have to experience it. And when you do, you suddenly click. 'This is it', will be the words that you mutter. If you have got used to living under pressure, you may have forgotten how this felt. You will realise that by returning to this state, it is the natural state where happiness and success flow more easily.

We will go through the practical and theocratical ways for you to adopt and learn to experience this state of being in the present with inner peace in your everyday life.

We must remember we were born in nature's purest form. We have lost the connection with Mother Nature as we grew up. We have lost touch with ourselves at the very core of our souls and the fundamental reality of the universe. We need to unlearn some of the behaviours that are destructive to our present lives.

Later in this book, you will learn how to return to that state.

REDEFINING SUCCESS

"Roads were made for journeys, not destinations".

-Confucius

Have you thought about what success actually looks like for you?

Even if you have already got out of the rat race and running your own business this still applies to you. You thought, to work for somebody else no longer served your mental well-being or perhaps you wanted to show someone you could do better?

Whatever the reason you are in your own business, it is time to cut the crap and discover what's really inside you.

If you are still fantasising with the idea of getting rich quick so that you can have a celebrity-like lifestyle and that is what is driving you, then you and I really need to talk.

You may have set a vision, goals and purpose for your business. You may have detailed plans and strategies on how you are going to grow your business or make it thrive. You may have your own financial goal you set which you want to achieve through the success of your business.

There is nothing wrong with that.

In fact, goal setting is very important in any personal

development programs. For most life coaches and consultants, this is one of the first things to do when we first work with a client. We explain the importance of setting goals and the consequence of not having one.

We help set this goal based on a client's values, aspirations and purpose of the business as well as personal life as we encourage them to imagine where they want to see themselves in one year, three years or five years' time.

I personally use the analogy of a sailing boat which sets sail without a destination and explains how, without setting a destination in advance, the boat will only drift and gets lost in the ocean. Setting financial goals and wealth goals are also important if you want to be comfortable in your old age instead of constantly worrying about money.

In many cases, clients had not thought about their ultimate goal of their life.

I might ask the client to imagine them on their death bed or sometimes called a rocking chair test, for the purpose of defining what their authentic self is here for on this earth and or to discover their true purpose. This might take some time, but by doing this, they are able to instinctively see more clearly what their destination is and therefore what they need to do today.

This is an important step in starting a personal development journey as this aligns oneself with the purpose and true self.

As a business and personal consultant, my job is not just to help set goals for two to five years. It is my job to help my clients to find their true purpose. Somewhere deep inside, we have a dream or vision. We might have forgotten about this or have dismissed it as impossible. This vision could be something a lot bigger than simply attaining success in your field.

It could be more to do with making a difference, having an impact or creating a change that affects, not just your life but many others that you care. That may be where your vision of success really lies. When you discover your true purpose and you start walking towards it, an extraordinary personal transformation can begin.

Even if you don't find your purpose straightaway, reconnecting with yourself and focusing on achieving inner peace will help you discover it in due course.

Setting the right goal is crucial, however, I believe it needs to be done with caution.

Over 600,000 new businesses get started in the UK each

year and many more are considering doing the same. Over 90% of the businesses are sole entrepreneurship which does not employ any staff. Many pluck up their courage to leave their 9-5 job or a position of being an employee to start their journey of entrepreneurship with great aspiration and self-belief from a desire for more success and a better life.

And the majority decide to do this for the reasons of wanting to earn more money, being their own boss, doing what they love, following their passion etc.

So how do you define success? Would you consider yourself to be successful when your business turns over a specific amount of revenue? Or is it the net profit you are concerned about?

Let's look at how we define success. The Oxford dictionary defines success as;

1.0 The accomplishment of an aim or purpose.

1.1 The attainment of fame, wealth, or social status.

1.2A person or thing that achieves desired aims or attains fame, wealth, etc.

2 The good or bad outcome of an undertaking.

Although the word success can also be used negatively, the majority of the times we use the word 'success' as something good. It is normally related to social status and wealth and for most business owners this remains to be something to aim for.

However, deep down each one of us have different perspectives of what 'personal' success actually represents. What success means to Sarah could completely differ from that of John's. For example, for Sarah, success might mean that growing her business and taking it public, jetting off to major cities in first-class and doing more lucrative deals. But for John, success might mean having the freedom of time to spend with his loved ones.

You might define success with the amount of money one earns rather than how much free time one has. You might be thinking of having both time and money is how you define success. You might also define success by how many people you have helped in your business.

Therefore, when we make a comment or have thoughts on someone's success, we base this on our own definition of success. Likewise, if someone else's success is not how you define success, it becomes irrelevant to you.

Social media has become a place where some people

showcase their life in technicolour. It is hard not to be influenced by other people's idea of success and to make a mistake of thinking, that is what you ought to accomplish to be successful.

Many people compete subconsciously against each other by over concerning themselves with how much others have in material wealth, how others spend their time or whom they mingle with and define success with it. Some people who are eager to keep up with this trend of material-gathering are prepared to go into debt to have the latest gadgets, cars and other things. Often the pleasure of attaining such items are short-lived and people are left with the repayment of loans and credit card debts which in itself can become a source of stress.

Interestingly, many wealthy business owners do not define success as having a lot of money. According to some research[*4] into wealthy people, it is found that they do not consider themselves successful because they are rich or powerful.

"In my opinion, true success should be measured by how happy you are."

-Richard Branson

Perhaps they have become successful because their

definition of success was more to do with happiness. It could be that what is important for some is personal fulfilment or gaining recognition. Our ultimate goal surely is to be happy and that is what we want for our children and everyone else, right?

We know from many research findings on lottery winners that money alone does not make you happy.

It doesn't mean, however you should stop pursuing money. Money is a 'tool'. It brings more freedom and choices. More freedom to use your time in different ways. Money not only brings freedom to us but can also be exchanged in many ways to help others. I will talk more about money and wealth later in this book. But for now, let's stick with the meaning of success. Do we want to help others? Do we want to make a difference in society?

If you are going to set goals for your business or your mission in life, set them by defining success in such a way that goes beyond what you want for yourself.

When you set your goal, rather than just setting a specific amount of money by such and such date, expand your goal to describe what exactly you will do with it by such and such date.

Because while making a profit is the purpose of a business, its purpose also is an accomplishment of its mission. It is understandable that it is normal for us to create business plans and sales target based on turnovers and profits, and to define the profitability of the business that way. Because that is how the business world operates in most instances. Bank managers and investors are usually interested in the profitability and the return on investments.

There is nothing wrong with that and I still believe it is an important way to measure your business performance. It is understandable if you think that is the only 'proper' way to measure performance as that is how we have learned to measure it.

But that is not the only way. It is also okay to set your business goals and in many cases a personal goal for entrepreneurs by how many people you intend to delight or how much difference you are going to make in someone's life, group, organisation or perhaps animals and nature depending on the type of business you are running.

For example, if you have set the business plan for it to turnover a certain amount of revenue this year, perhaps for your investors or your bank, translate this into the 'value' that the business will be providing. For example, if you are in the business of selling a device to save time, such as a robotic vacuum cleaner, measure how many hours, by selling this device, your business is going to save for each household per year rather than how many units you are planning sell.

In their brochure, Ocado says they have given UK families over 150,000,000 hours of free time back through their online grocery shopping and delivery service. That is such a great way to measure the success and the value the business exists to provide.

Let's look at another example. Climate change should be on everyone's agenda. Your business can be one of those businesses that tackle this issue and make a huge contribution.

Your success through your business can be measured by how much pollution you help reduce by using a different source, how much plastic you helped to eliminate by changing packaging or how much water you saved by manufacturing in an ethical way.

"I have always found that my view of success has been iconoclastic: success to me is not about money or status or fame, it's about finding a livelihood that brings me joy and self-sufficiency and a sense of contributing to the world."

– Anita Roddick

Anita Roddick founded the Body Shop partly because she did not agree with the amount of money being spent on the packaging by major cosmetic brands at the time. This sort of success story and having goals to make an impact on the planet and society is not just for the corporate giants. It is also for small businesses and entrepreneurs.

By defining success in this way rather than the value in money, you bring your business closer to your heart and soul and perhaps to the heart and soul to the people you employ in your business as well as customers you serve.

You will feel better when recognising that you are in business to provide value rather than just to make money. The money will follow anyway.

This way of thinking will also help you break through a limiting belief because you no longer need to feel guilty for wanting more money if you ever did.

When you have finished setting the goal and it's clear, you will get used to measuring success by how much value you have provided. Then you will be ready to come back to living in the present.

Why live in the present and not focus on your goals daily? you might think.

Many business leaders and motivational books encourage you to keep your future vision in your mind at all times and focus on that.

But if we try to live in anticipation of our success constantly or the money it is supposed to bring, perhaps glancing at our vision board while we stress over our loan payments, we are not actually attracting success the way we should do. Just because abundant universal energy does not flow like that.

You may even have attained some amount of success already and want to take your business to the next level. The rule is the same. While your mind is focusing on the future, you are not living in the present and therefore you might be missing out on the important events and life itself as they happen.

In the society where we got used to seeing other people's live streaming and live feeds, we must not forget the drama that is constantly unfolding and simple pleasures within our own life.

If the science proves that success follows happiness, then we must shift our focus on here and now and find happiness and fulfilment in the present.

This sounds so counterintuitive for business owners and entrepreneurs as we are chasers of success. We set goals to accomplish them. We take actions towards our goals and make ourselves accountable for meeting the deadlines.

But whatever level you achieve this year, you will want more next year and so it goes on. Just like the never-ending 'to-do' list. It is more about actually feeling the pleasure, fun and fulfilment in being part of the journey called life and when you stop worrying about the outcome, that is when success seems to arrive.

Take time now before reading any further to consider how you define success and the detailed description of the success you want to accomplish. We will then move on to the exciting phase of learning how to change our energy frequency to get back in harmony with the universe.

HOW YOU LIVE

**"Your beliefs become your thoughts,
Your thoughts become your words,
Your words become your actions,
Your actions become your habits,
Your habits become your values,
Your values become your destiny."**

— Mahatma Gandhi

5 STEPS TO SMARTZEN

Now your visions, purpose and goals are taken care of and your success redefined, you are ready to enjoy the journey of SmartZen way.

There are five areas you need to look at to harmonise in order to reach the state of being that empowers yourself to manifest better health, happiness and success. These elements work together to create not only the harmony and balance in your life but to accelerate the results enormously.

If you imagine yourself sitting by a river flowing with pure spring water on a warm sunny day. The sunshine reflecting on the water making it sparkle. No living thing can survive without water. This water is the pure essence and what keeps us alive. Now imagine that the water is the energy and flowing through the channel. Imagine that riverbed itself is our body and mind.

If you create obstacles by throwing large rocks or a dam, the water does not flow smoothly. If you contaminate the water with toxins, this affects what can grow here, do you want your fish to flourish or flounder? In the same way, if we block the flow of the energy or contaminate the energy with negative thoughts, we will not help ourselves to channel the energy through us effectively.

Water flows very fast in a river without obstacles. In the same way, you can help the energy to flow more easily by removing mental obstacles that might be in your way right now.

Contrary to the popular belief in the law of attraction, just by thinking about what you want, adjusting your thoughts to that of positivity and meditating daily to maintain calm mind does not necessarily bring abundance to yourself.

If you have been meditating for a while, or have a vision board already set up and have been talking positive affirmation to yourself but have not yet seen the kind of result you have been looking forward to, it could be because you have only been working on the surface of one or two areas of your life.

For example, you might have been focusing on creating wealth, but have been neglecting your health by not eating well. Or you might have been focusing on feeling happier but had not been considering the effect your living environment has been having on you.

But when you work on all five elements of your life, you will feel it as if everything has just clicked in the right place.

This might feel like a surge of energy filling up your entire body.

Or it might be that you notice that suddenly if you could hear a tune of your own vibration in complete harmony.

That is when a transformation of your entire life will occur more easily.

Think of this as a five-piece music band playing a beautiful piece of music together. Each instrument plays an important role in making an ensemble of music. Each gives out a different flavour of the tune and each instrument can play an entire piece alone and it might sound okay. But when the band gets together to play that piece and in harmony, the music is synchronised and beautiful.

Call it 'Torvill and Dean' or 'Kevin Keegan and John Toshack' of your internal teams dancing and playing perfectly in perfect sync. You can create your own awesome team.

The five elements I am going to work with you are:

Physicality

Place

People

Pace

Purpose

As we go through step by step to restore each element of your life and start re-tuning, you will realise how they are interrelated to each other. You will understand that whatever you want in life will be manifested more easily when all elements are in harmony. You will also discover what areas had been blocking the energy. It is very possible that as soon as you re-tune your energy to the right frequency in the areas that had the block, you will feel a complete shift in your well-being.

As you get used to being in tune with the self, and that becomes the norm, you will feel uncomfortable being any other state. Returning to that state will become easier as you practice and work on all areas of your life.

Physicality - Beginning the Restoration

What we eat and how we treat our body depends on how we view ourselves. Without having to go back to your childhood when you had no control over what you were fed, you are now old enough to decide what you put in your precious body. Not only the nutrition for your body, but you are also in a position to decide how to treat your body.

Every new year, you may decide on a new year's resolution which might include improving your well-being. You might have said 'I am going on a healthy diet'. Or I am going to cut down on alcohol' or 'I am going to join a gym.'

If you have been able to keep up with what you have decided at the beginning of the year, you have a greater chance of transforming your health. But for most people, a new year's resolution or decision to change things end in a few short weeks of making that decision.

One of the important ideas to adapt is to understand that your health is the result of your mental state.

Our body responds to the state of your mind. Let's take a look at how your physical body responds to stress as a typical example.

According to a research*5 conducted by the Mental Health Foundation in the UK, due to stress;

46% of people ate too much or ate unhealthily

29% reported that they started drinking or increased their drinking

16% reported that they started smoking or increased their smoking.

When you feel stress, a stress hormone called cortisol is released. Cortisol plays an important role in a number of things your body does to respond to stress. One of them is managing how your body uses carbohydrates, protein and fats. As your stress hormone is your natural alarm system, which is triggered when you feel stressed, your body responds to protect you.

Some of its responses include boosting energy to cope with stress and to restore balance in your body. In order for the body to boost energy, it needs to raise the blood sugar level, which is used for energy so, it demands carbohydrates which is turned in to sugar or glucose.

If you crave for cakes and bread such as doughnuts, muffins and cookies when you are stressed, that might be when your body is responding to stress.

If there is any excess glucose left in your body excess, your body turns it into fats and put it into long term storage for future use. And as a result, you might find yourself gaining weight you don't want.

Even if you don't recognise yourself as suffering from stress, you might be naturally starting to crave food that is high in calorie or more carbohydrates. If you are not happy, not content, experiencing despair, or whatever state your mind is in, your body is constantly adjusting itself to cope without you having to think about it.

One of the reasons people who vowed to eat healthily and go on a healthy diet fail to sustain the habit is because they have not tackled the real cause of excessive or unhealthy eating and drinking.

When you are consciously trying hard to choose healthy food, but you end up reaching for the chocolate muffin or a glass of gin and tonic, and you feel guilty afterwards, you start a vicious circle of negative thoughts.

In Japan, contrary to what most Western people think, people eat a lot of food high in calories. Japanese people love sweet things as it is usual to add sugar during cooking. While most people think of raw fish and sushi as the main food in Japanese cuisine, most Japanese people eat sushi less than once a week. Some of the common dishes such as tempura and katsu are deep-fried.

Each year Japan consumes over 8600 tons of rice which are the main source of carbohydrates. People in Japan also eat wheat-based noodles as a large part of their diet.

And Japanese cuisine is not just what Japanese people eat. European and other Asian cuisines are just as popular. And only about 4% of the population consider themselves as either vegetarian or vegan. So, the Japanese are as much meat-eaters as British.

But according to the stats published by WHO, (the world health organisation) in 2014, the average BMI (body mass index) for Japanese was lower at 22.6 in comparison to the UK of 27.3 and the US of 28.8.

So, what can be learned from the Japanese habits of eating?

Like many healthy eating advice, I could talk about how much tofu and miso was used in a Japanese meal and adding seaweed and raw fish could enhance your healthy diet. But my aim here is not to convert your taste in food.

Of course, the benefits of soy are being recognised by the West much more than before. And fermented pickles, for example, another important part of the Japanese food that is very beneficial to your body has been gaining recognition as a part of a healthy diet in the West.

But what I want to focus on here is not what you eat but HOW you eat.

Because there is a difference between the Japanese way of eating and the British way for example.

To explain this, I first have to introduce you to the Japanese philosophy of eating food with your eyes.

No, I don't mean it literally.

The Japanese take much care in the presentation of each dish as the quality and the taste of the food itself. The importance of aesthetics is found not only in the cuisine but in the design of traditional architecture, garden and art and some modern counterpart.

The notion of food is for survival and a source of nutrition is put aside, the philosophy is in the enjoyment and the appreciation of the food that is presented before your eyes.

You might have an experience like this when you have come across a dish which has been prepared with care and attention, not only during the process of cooking but also when it is dished up.

In the last 15-20 years or so in Britain, this movement towards the good aesthetic presentation of food developed rapidly and can be seen in certain restaurants. These were first classed as 'gourmet'.

But over the last decade, even in pubs, we have seen creative ways to present food from chips being delivered in a wired cage on a rustic chopping board.

I would like you to think of when and how you enjoy a meal which is beautifully presented. Picture such an occasion in your mind, in a relaxed atmosphere, perhaps in the company of people you love. Your dish is beautiful to look at, but the volume of the food itself is not necessarily that huge. It might be that a small piece of meat, fish or vegetable is sitting in the middle of a large plate garnished with other food which has contrasting colours, almost as if it is an art form.

When you look at something beautiful, this time your body reacts in another way. Because your brain is wired to activate pleasure-inducing transmitters to raise your positive emotion, not stress.

Beauty is therefore linked with pleasure.

Feeling pleasure as opposed to feeling stressed can be enhanced by looking at something beautiful. And this includes the food you eat.

The secondary effect of feeling pleasure is that it leads to feeling contentment. When you feel happy you feel content in the present state. You do not need to stuff yourself with a large volume of food. When you see beautiful food, and you cherish and receive this with pleasure and appreciation, you take care of the process of eating and digesting the food.

Your stomach gets the message of feeling content, thus avoiding overindulging.

I give SmartZen Food Presentation Award for dishes that are beautifully presented for our eyes. If you are interested in checking out the photos of these, please follow me on www.instagram.com/yumironi or #smartzenfood.

Even when you are preparing your own food to serve yourself, keep this in mind. You do not need to spend hours creating an awesome looking dish. Your everyday meal can be presented with an aesthetic in mind and in a relatively simple way.

If you find yourself craving for sweets or junk food, remember that it is your body's response to the status of your mind. Before reaching for that banana muffin or an extra-large glass of wine, ask yourself what it is that is happening in your mind right now.

Did you just encounter a situation that made you angry, frustrated, under pressure or anxious?

As you go through the process of adopting SmartZen philosophy, you will be better equipped to deal with the emotional roller coasters that have ruled your eating habits until now.

Eating is a basic need for human existence. It is your friend, not a foe. Make friends with your food and let it be a source of joy and happiness not a reason for unwanted weight gain or illnesses that can follow chronic stress.

Rejuvenate or Produce

I have lived in the UK for many years but there is something I cannot get in the UK that I still miss. It is one thing I ensure I have it every time I visit Japan. I have tried to re-create this by adapting what we have in the UK, but this has not been possible.

You have visited Japan you did this as one of the touristy things to do or simply out of necessity.

It is indeed doing this is classed as our basic need and we in the developed country are lucky to have this readily available to us albeit in a different form.

What am I talking about?

I cannot get it in the UK, but all developed countries have in different forms and it is also to do with meeting our basic needs?

I am talking about taking a bath.

When you think about having or taking a bath, we do this as a routine for maintaining personal hygiene. Indeed, running water has enabled us to keep ourselves and our clothes clean.

We are lucky to have fresh water delivered to our home and most of us are able to cleanse our body in a shower or bath every day.

Most of us have got used to taking a shower as opposed to having a bath and in some modern homes, they don't even install a bathtub in their bathroom in order to save space.

But bathing can be a therapeutic experience.

In recent years, spas have become a major trend for people to use to rejuvenate and relax away from their busy lifestyles. Many fitness gyms and hotels have got on to this idea of combining health, fitness and relaxation to attract customers.

Often you find jacuzzi or thermal bath beautifully created in a relaxing setting where you find yourself immersed in warm water shared by complete strangers.

The increase in popularity of spas is not surprising when we see people leading very busy lives and need the right environment to relax.

In Japan, especially in major cities like Tokyo, people lead as busy lives as any of their Western counterparts. It is not unusual for normal office workers to clock up 50-60 hours a week. One survey said that more than a quarter of companies require their workers to work 80 hours a week. This is often on top of spending 1-2 hours each day commuting on trains.

Japan has a culture of not taking paid leave and feeling guilty for doing so. That is why the Japanese government is considering placing a cap on working hours to prevent 'karoshi' a term now well known in the business industry, as death by overworking.

In such a working culture where many people are stressed each day, one thing the Japanese are good at is to relieve stress. Going to a karaoke box and signing your hearts out is one such method but taking a relaxing moment each day bathing is another.

If you have visited Japan as a tourist or on a business trip and only had an experience of staying in modern hotels, you may not have come across this type of bath. As most business hotels are designed in the Western style with an ensuite bathroom just like any hotel room you find in Europe.

Baths in a Japanese home is very different from that of the West. As a start, the toilet is never found in the same room as a bathtub. Often the toilet is in the vicinity but located separately from the bathroom itself.

The bathtub is usually deep so that when you sit in the water you can immerse yourself in it up to your shoulders. The water is normally filled or kept at a temperature of about 38°C. In many homes, the bathtub itself is equipped with a device that both fills the bath with hot water, stops automatically when it reaches an ideal water level and the water is kept to a required temperature just by a touch of a button.

But the main difference in bathing is not about the design of the bathtub or the technology but the way people have a bath.

In Japan, you wash outside the bath before getting in the bathtub so that you are not soaking in your own scum. The water remains clean so it can be used by other members of the family in turn, saving water and energy.

I suppose not many people like the idea of bathing in your own dirt anyway so, in the West the popularity of taking a shower instead increased together with the ecological reasons.

But having a bath in a Japanese home is a bit like having a spa in your own home. After cleansing yourself, dipping into the hot water in a steaming bathroom can give you a sense of serenity. As you sit in a hot water and immersing your body fully up to your shoulders, your muscles start to relax, and your mind starts to unravel the tension you had been feeling all day. Here in your own company, you can reflect and restore peace as your physical body is rejuvenated. It is a therapeutic experience.

Bathing is a large part of Japanese philosophy. Buddhist temples had bathhouses where monks used for purification. In the 6th century, bathhouses were initially for the exclusive use for monks but eventually, it was opened up for the public as only the wealthy had a bath in their own home.

This culture of communal bathing still exists and is an important past time in Japan. The communal bathing in hot spring water has been established for centuries and called 'Onsen' where people go and soak in for therapeutic quality of volcanic hot spring. This slightly resembles the Western jacuzzi in spas, where you share the bath with strangers. But Onsen is still a bathhouse and swimming suits are not permitted. You must be naked to use the facility and in most places, there are separate baths for men and women. If you go into the deep countryside, you may still find an Onsen where men and women share the same bath with complete strangers.

Whenever I go back to Japan, I often look for Onsen where they have a bath outside the building, usually in the garden or a side of the hill overlooking the valley. During the most recent visit to Kyoto, the ancient capital of Japan, I had the pleasure of visiting a beautiful Onsen with a good friend of mine. It was a winter day and snow was falling. As we took a local single-track train up the mountain away from the city, we were invited to the scenery of the mountain covered with snow. There stood the Onsen house where the bathwater was collected from the mountain spring rich in minerals.

There were three or four baths in different temperatures you could try but the most beautiful one was that of the garden bath. The bath was surrounded by a beautiful Japanese garden and a fantastic view of the valley and the mountains beyond. The bath was the size of a small swimming pool and a few women were already there. As we sat in the hot water, where the air temperature was near zero, snow started to fall. It was a pure tranquillity.

You may think it is a little weird to share a bath, naked with complete strangers or even with your friends. But there is no need to get hung up about our body and aesthetic of nakedness. There is nothing embarrassing about it.

By the way, in Japan, it is normal for a family to share the baths. When children are small, one of the parents has a bath with them. If they have a big enough bath it is not unusual for the whole family to bath together. Children grow up seeing their parent's naked body and other people's body in Onsen.

It is totally normal in Japan.

Children naturally grow up knowing there are many different shapes and sizes, new and old and there is nothing to hide or feel ashamed about.

Actually, communal bathing is not just a Japanese idea. The ancient Romans and Greeks were also enjoying communal bathing in their thermae. They used it not just for cleansing but for socialising and reading.

So how can we adopt this way of using bathing for purification, restoring our body and reflection in our own everyday life when we cannot visit a Spa or an Onsen on a daily basis?

One of the things you can do is to learn to use the bath at home in a different way and is to think of bathing as a process of recovery of body and mind. Instead of using a bath only when you feel unwell or cold, create a regular meeting place of body and mind.

Use your bath not only as a place to maintain personal hygiene, but to realign your senses, stimulate your immune system and unwind your busy mind.

Make it a routine to give yourself a lymphatic massage, too. You can use a mitten with a rough surface to massage your body in the opposite direction of the lymphatic passages.

The lymphatic system is an awesome system that can help most people immensely. The lymphatic system is a network in your body similar to veins. But instead of blood, it transports lymph which travels all over your body. Its job is to detect and attack bad things in your body. If more lymph is needed, your body sends a signal for more lymph to be made in your spleen or your tonsils. The healthy immune system is maintained when your lymphatic system is working in the most efficient way. It is like having your own army of soldiers ready to combat enemies day or night.

Sometimes this immune system could do with help from you. Sometimes the lymph gets blocked or not flowing well. So that lymph can flow in well throughout your body so that it can do their job well. In the transformational program, I teach lymphatic massage for face and body that you can do yourself. I often give this gentle massage to my children, too when they are feeling under the weather in order to boost their immune system.

You can do this massage without the use of mitten. But I personally use the mitten for two things. One for massage and the other to exfoliate my skin thereby stimulating circulation and helping the renewal process of my skin surface.

Lymphatic massage can help reduce the chance of you suffering from minor colds and viruses; it **helps your body fight off infection** and speeds up healing and recovery from illness. It also improves your metabolism to burn calories more efficiently.

I believe it is a safe massage for anyone to do at home, but if you suffer from a heart condition, are on medication or have any other chronic conditions, it is best to check with your doctor first.

Being Moderately Active

We cannot talk about physical health without talking about exercises I suppose.

For someone who has joined and quitted the gym a few times, I am not the right person to endorse joining a gym. Having said that I think many gyms offer many options to suit many different methods of exercises including yoga classes, which cater very well for the majority of busy people. Not to mention, it's a good way of making a commitment to those activities.

The key to exercising regularly is choosing something you enjoy but it does not happen without certain discipline.

I find it interesting that although Japanese people are quite self-conscious and tend to live a more healthy life, you do not find as many fitness gyms as there are in the UK.

It is true that Japan has a limited land space in comparison to the UK. Even though it is about the same size in the land surface, as the Japanese islands are mainly volcanic mountains, only about 30% of the land is suitable for habitation. About 10% of that is taken up by the infrastructure, so its 130 million people are living side by side gathered in the 20% of the entire land, making Tokyo as one of the most densely populated cities in the world.

Fitness gym is a growing business and there are about 7,000 of them in the UK. In comparison to this, in Japan, there are about 5,000 gyms for twice as many populations. This means there is one gym available for every 2,500 to 3,000 people in Japan. Imagine your local gym trying to cater to 3,000 members. It's crazy.

It might be that the trend has not yet hit Japan, it might be that there is not enough space to build a gym with a good facility like David Lloyds. Or it might be that there is simply not enough demand.

When you go to Japan, you do not see many people in their fitness gear jogging or running in town. It is actually dangerous to be running on the pavement anyway because it is not easy to avoid people. People tend to do and expect people to do the running on a suitable sports facility.

Coming back to exercising itself, there is so many conflicting advice about keeping yourself fit nowadays. For example, the relationship between cardio exercise and increase of free radicals which are damaging. It is not surprising that people get confused. I think it is true that as you get older your body slows down.

I am not sure about going to a gym to lose weight though. Your body burns calories, so you tend to top up the calorie by eating as much if not more to sustain that level of energy-burning routine.

When the government advises us to do regular exercise, it doesn't exactly help. It is not the exercise itself that promotes well-being. The only thing I believe is true is that when you have exercised your body, you feel better. That is why going for a brisk walk when you are feeling low, works.

People say I should do some exercise to burn off the calorie after having a big Sunday lunch. But the fact is that going for a short walk does not do much for burning calories. From what I heard; you have to walk 5-6 miles to burn off 500 calories for average people. And that is not walking at a leisurely pace. That is by a brisk walk.

In fact, it is more beneficial to exercise before eating, because your body takes the nutrients it needs from the food more effectively by replenishing rather than storing.

I am not against the idea of exercising to lose weight, but the point is that exercising should be fun, makes you strong and not a chore.

Exercises help your body releases chemicals called endorphin which is commonly known as natural pain relief. It can help reduce stress, anxiety and depression. It can improve sleep and self-esteem. The physical effects include strengthening of your heart, increasing energy, lowering of blood pressure, building bones, as well as reducing body fat and improving muscle tone.

The overall effect is that you feel better and healthier.

Exercise does not only have to happen in a sweaty gym though, but it can also be many different forms such as;

- Biking
- Dancing
- Gardening, mowing or raking
- Golf and walking the course
- Housework, especially sweeping, mopping, or vacuuming
- Jogging at a moderate pace
- Low-impact aerobics
- Playing tennis
- Swimming
- Walking
- Yoga
- Tai Chi
- Martial art

The point about exercise is having fun and helping your body and mind to stay strong and to maintain health. What better way to do this by killing two birds with one stone?

Treating housework such as hoovering and mopping as a form of exercise is a good way to get the cleaning done as part of a routine. Washing your car as fast as possible not only gets some work done but getting your heart pumping, which is good for you anyway. If you are hiring domestic help to do your housework and car washing, I suppose you have to find other ways to keep active.

I admit I am quite lazy. Most of the time I think about how to do things in the most efficient way. Basically, I try to think of ways to save time.

That is why I have created an exercise routine that incorporates meditation and physical movement. It is like a fusion of yoga, tai chi and martial art. This is easy to learn but highly effective. You can do this anywhere without the need of a mat or taking your shoes off. If you are interested in learning the routine, please check out our website.

A form of exercise we have not talked about that can be good cardio or stretch is sex. I have always thought of sex as a perfect exercise that works well for your mind as well as your body.

So how about a half an hour of karma sutra instead of hitting the gym?

You might find that your body and soul are lifted up higher than any places treadmills or cross trainers can take you.

Place - Home as A Sanctuary

The famous zen garden in Kyoto, Ryoanji temple is a very different walled garden to the sort of beautiful gardens you see in the Chelsea Flower Show. In fact, there are no plants other than moss in the garden apart from what is draping over the wall that surrounds the garden. But it is a garden not for sitting in but to look at.

The garden; a rectangular plot surrounded by walls is simply laid with grey gravel with fifteen large rocks clustered into small groups sitting on a patch of moss of various shapes and sizes seemingly placed randomly. The rocks are positioned in such a way that whatever angle you look at the garden from, one cannot view all of the rocks at the same time. Some people interpret this as a representation of a human being.

Zen gardens normally found in a garden of Zen Buddhist temples. You can sit in front of it to meditate, contemplate and restore your inner peace. There is no visible distraction to take your attention away from what's in the present. And the garden itself symbolises the human nature made up of blood, bone and flesh represented by water, rocks and plants.

Home is a shelter where you are protected from the elements and a safe place where you can spend your time restoring your energy. It can be a place where you get relief from the pressure of the outside world and away from other demands placed upon you much of the time if not daily.

To live in a home where you cannot feel peace and restorative energy is 'suffering'. Most of us in the developed county is lucky enough to live in a sturdy building where a wolf cannot huff and puff and blow it down.

We have built, well not personally, but a shelter where most of our basic needs are met. Clean running water, warmth, cleanness and safety combined with technology that makes our lives easier.

But some people have created and are living in an environment with clutter and disorganised chaos. Or sharing their space with people they have a permanent conflict with. No wonder we are not restoring our body and mind overnight when we go home.

Home is such an important stress-relieving element that

many people seem to miss. This could be that we get used to it. When we see the same clutter day after day, it no longer registers and you become numb to how much it is actually blocking positive energies around the home.

The Five Elements of Nature

In Feng Shui which is the art of arranging your home and office originally from China, we can use the universal energy to stimulate or change the aspects of our lives by being conscious of the energy in our home. It recognises the flow of energy and directs it with the help of five natural elements. There are five elements we recognise as energy in nature which is water, fire, wood, metal and earth. Most homes have these elements but you may not have placed your furniture, ornaments or decorations without giving much thought to these.

While I am not an expert in Feng Shui, the essence of this is something I have always tried to incorporate in my home decor and garden designs which is simple for anyone to adopt.

If you think of your home as a place where you collect good energy to replenish your energy so that you can restore your body and mind well each time you spend in it, you can begin to see the benefits of being a little more conscious of how you set up your environment for relaxation, comfort as well as for working environment. By placing certain things made of one of the elements, you strengthen that energy and therefore enhance the effect.

For example, if you want to enhance your health and wealth, find the directions in your home which is the East for Health and South East for wealth to bring the right energy to that area.   East and South-East are associated with the element of wood. So, in order to strengthen the wood, you can place items that enhance the element which is water. You may place a plant (wood) or aquarium (water) or a water feature which strengthen the energy. But avoid items made of metal or a candle (fire) which destroys wood, and so on.

Here are the direction and the aspects of your life and direction and elements associated with each.

Direction	Element	Life Area
East	Wood	Health
South East	Wood	Wealth/Accumulation
South	Fire	Recognition/Fame
South West	Earth	Relationship/Marriage
West	Metal	Children/Projects
North West	Metal	People/Contracts
North	Water	Career/Journey
North East	Earth	Wisdom/Knowledge

Now consider what element will enhance the area of your life by consulting the cycle below.

The enhancing and damaging cycles run like this.

Wood is helped by water.

Water is helped by Metal

Metal is helped by Earth

Earth is helped by Fire

Fire is helped by Wood.

Wood is harmed by Metal

Metal is harmed by Fire

Fire is harmed by water

Water is harmed by Earth

Earth is harmed by Wood

And so on. Enjoy moving things around and see if you can use the energy from the universe to enhance a particular aspect of your life.

Energy Everywhere

The biggest change in our life for the last 20 years was not really the shift in how we see the world and finding the parallels between Physics and Eastern philosophy. Nor it is that more people have begun to practise meditation all over the world.

What really transformed our lives is the advancement of technology.

In the digitally connected society, we are so isolated from our own self. Every minute and every second of the day we are bombarded with external stimuli that take our attention away from our meditative state.

We pay more attention to sad stories of people in the news and social media whom we probably would never meet. Yet, we do not necessarily know what is happening in our own psyche, our family or neighbourhood.

We have got used to working in disharmony. Disharmony has become the norm. There is disharmony in the world between religions and countries. There is so much disharmony in politics. There is disharmony in society. Disharmony between genders and there is disharmony within family units. No wonder we are exhausted. We have become numb to disharmony and have learnt to accept it.

This is very disturbing. The technology has brought about convenience, fast speed and all the good things, right? We don't have to wash clothes and dishes with our hands any more so have created more time to do other things, right? We can travel to places much faster than ever before, so we save time here too, right?

Machines do the work humans used have to do by hand, so that we reduced manual work in all sectors from manufacturing to office work so that we save time to spend with our loved ones, right?

Don't get me wrong. I am very much fond of technology. Technology has made it possible to speak to someone on the other side of the earth for free, for example. Technology eliminated a lot of the manual work I used to do for business accounts.

I enjoy online shopping because I don't have to fight the crowds, queue up or make the decision to buy stuff then and then. I can research other shops with a touch of a few keys to check out their prices for the same product and so on.

The technology was meant to make things more efficient, help us and make our lives better. Technologies are being used to save lives and the planet.

But we are more distracted as well as disrupted by technology than ever before.

According to the study by the Mental Health Foundation in 2018, 74% of people have felt so stressed in the past year that they have been overwhelmed or unable to cope. 12% of people who reported high levels of stress answered that 'feeling like they need to respond to messages instantly was a stressor'.

What are we doing to ourselves?

As we continue the steps in restoring harmony in your life; we start by decluttering your social media and email inbox.

Decluttering Digital Life

Digital technology must be managed in your life to get the most out it. Just like any physical rubbish, it can soon build up to a mountain of trash, which will be overwhelming to manage.

Instruction:

1: Open your personal email's inbox and unsubscribe all the emails from businesses, shopping sites, promotional items, discount sites that meet at least one of the following criteria;

    A. You have not opened
    B. Contents are no longer relevant
    C. You can always sign up again

Don't just delete the emails. Open the email and click unsubscribe link. It is usually at the bottom of the email. Sometimes it says, 'manage your subscription'. Do this until you go back for three months. As you go through this process, keep a memo of the name of the companies you unsubscribed from. This will give you a mental picture of;

   1. How many companies have been distracting your attention.
   2. How much you are suffering from FOMO.

If you manage more than one email address do this for all of them.

Organising Inbox

If you have not already done so, it is a good time to organise your emails into categories.

Alternatively, have at least three email addresses for three different purposes. One for newsletters, special discounts from shops etc. The second one is for business purpose, suppliers, networks. And the third one is for your personal use. If you only give your personal email address to important people, you will not get them mixed up with junk mail etc.

For your clients and customers, I highly recommend you set up an autoresponder with an email marketing program so that your customers are communicated through a separate channel. You could also use a CRM system (customer relationship management) so that you can keep track of the dialogue with each customer as the needs arise.

Controlling Social Media

Social media have changed so much over the last few years and more businesses are using the platforms for promoting businesses. If you are using social media to market your business, sometimes managing your personal profile as well as the business page is hard.

If you are finding it hard to promote your business openly and keeping your business activities separate from your personal profile, let me ask you why that is.

Sometimes when people start their own business on aside from what they do as the main job, they don't want their colleagues to be aware of this.

Or perhaps you deal in products that are not so ethical, might cause a conflict of interest or something you feel you cannot openly promote.

Sometimes you might have been using social media to let others know how well you are doing in your life and that you don't necessarily want people to know the reality of your life's journey.

This could be a big dilemma as a celebrity, influencer or entrepreneur.

But keeping up a separate persona can be a cause of stress in itself. If you are promoting your business through social media, remember that you will be known for the people you're connected to, the ideas you are immersed in, and what you care deeply about.

So, think again if you have discrepancies between your persona, (otherwise known as 'fake') you are trying to portray on social media and the real you.

Free from Home Energy Blockage

Now you have decluttered your inbox, social media and online activities, and discovered where you need to direct the energy in your home, it is time to get your home decluttered to let this energy flow like a dance.

When you start noticing how clutter can affect the state of your mind and wellbeing, you can see how important it is to energise the space where you place your physical body.

Since appearing in Netflix series, the Japanese tidying up expert Marie Kondo has highlighted the importance of having a home that is organised and clutter-free. She starts the decluttering process by asking the house its permission for her and her clients to do this. She teaches the client to express gratitude to each item for serving a useful life before disposing of it.

I love this idea and it is in line with my belief that the benefits of synchronising energy extends to your home and work environment. I will talk about the people who also live in your home in the next chapter but having less stuff in your house makes it easier to keep the place tidy which is logical.

How does clutter start in the first place when we were all born with no clothes or belonging when we first arrived on this earth?

Obviously, we have collected many items over the living years, and I know there might be many things you may find it hard to get rid of.

But to live a clutter-free life there are certain insights you need to have.

Do you come across people who are trying to be kind to you and offer you stuff they no longer want? Perhaps you receive emails from groups of people giving things away because it is better for the environment to recycle and reuse as much as possible instead of buying new.

It is often items in good condition, perhaps were expensive when they bought it or even still quite valuable second hand? This could be anything, like items of clothing, accessories like handbags, shoes, electrical goods or furniture. Then you think, well I suppose I could make use of that myself as it is a shame to throw it away. Then what happens is it gets transported into your living environment. You end up with the stuff you have not chosen yourself or that you don't exactly love but fills the space.

There are two things that might be happening here.

Your friend/family or the giver might be feeling guilty about disposing of an item that is perfectly in good condition. By giving it to you, they are relieving themselves of the guilt and pain that is associated with creating waste. Giving this item to you let them believe that they are a generous person who cares about others including the planet. They want to feel good inside themselves that's why they are offering you their stuff. Basically, they shift the responsibility of making the decision whether this lovely item should be thrown away on to you. If you refuse you would be the guilty party for creating waste in this world. That is why you being a good person want to give this item a second life by adopting it into your life.

See what's happening here?

Now I am not accusing anyone to be a bad person here. And I am sure sometimes you go 'well thanks, this is exactly what I need right now!', and then there is no problem.

But when you accept items that you did not acquire out of your own desire or choice, you bring a different kind of energy into your environment. Let's say you have accepted a piece of furniture like an armchair that was perfectly in good condition and functional as a chair but is not quite to your taste. It might not have been something you would choose to buy yourself if you saw it in a shop. But you had space for it. You did want a chair there one day, but you hadn't got around to getting one or finding one suitable. Now, this chair that someone else has chosen is sitting in your space. Now space is filled there is not a space left for what you want.

Think of items that you have acquired in this way and see if you feel that this item gives you a good vibe and create a sense of joy, peace and love. If they don't ask yourself why you have them in your life. Are they simply there to fill up space?

If your answer is because you would feel bad about throwing it away, then think about the reasons you might have acquired it in the first place.

I am all for recycling and reducing waste, but do not fill your life up with someone else's' rubbish unless it gives you joy, peace and good energy.

This is the same for acquiring new stuff. If you find yourself buying more clothes, shoes, kitchen stuff and gadgets when you can perfectly live without them, stop and ask yourself.

Am I creating clutter and contributing to the life of excess?

One of the things you might do when you go to a retreat, sabbatical or monastery for spiritual cleansing is learning to live with very minimal things.

It is surprising how little material things we actually need to feel safe, valued, and happy.

A lot of us, have got used to buying mass-produced items because they are affordable without thinking deeply enough where they came from and whether it is something we really need.

It is time to cleanse your home to let positive energy flow.

Make a start on decluttering your environment, surround yourself with only the items you love and care which bring joy and positive energy to you and your family.

Start living simply, let the loving energy flow in your home and your working space.

HOW YOU RELATE

People - Your Social Network

Your social life is not only online through social media. Sometimes the people you spend most of the time with could be the source of great stress, unhappiness and despair while others are a source of great joy, fun, inspiration and love.

It is not easy to declutter your social network like you declutter your home as you are dealing with humans and you cannot just deliver them to a charity shop just because you have finished with them.

But that is why it is also so important to reflect on what is working and what is not working for you. It is not unusual to grow out of someone or place or a lifestyle you got accustomed to. As you grow spiritually and mentally, sometimes you find that you have out-grown your existing network as a whole. This might be just because you are vibrating at a higher frequency and no longer resonating with those people and their values and aspirations. Or it could be that now you have grown, you can see through the BS you used to put up with.

Even though you may have hundreds of friends on your social network, most of us keep a few close friends that we regularly connect with and consider to be true friends. True friendship is a relationship where two people love each other enough to be available to each other in times of needs, as well as a source of inspiration, energy and the occasional ass kicking that you can benefit from.

The key is to identify the source of disharmony in your life which might be related to your social network. You can then become aware of how much of that relationship contributes to your overall happiness or unhappiness.

Being aware is the start of adjusting your frequency to universal energy. You will feel that if there is disharmony in your relationship to individuals, you will also become aware of how much or little a particular relationship has been influencing your well-being as a whole.

If you are single and have been looking for a suitable partner or a life's companion, it works in exactly the same way.

First of all, you have to create a space in your mind and your heart for someone to be manifested in your life. Focus on channelling the universal energy and find happiness in the present, then you will attract people to your life that you will want to share your life with.

All the time you are feeling unhappy about not having a lover, you are at the same time reinforcing that energy to go around. Equally, if you look for someone to arrive out of 'needs', you may bring someone to you that does not quite fit into enhancing the well-being of all concerned.

Like success, love also seems to arrive when you are in a happy state first.

Have a think about the people you come in regular contact with at work, at home and in your community. Review the relationship you have with each of them and rate the relationship according to the level of good feelings you get from the relationship itself. Do you feel uplifted when you spend time with them? Does the relationship you have with them contribute to your growth, their growth or both?

You don't have to do anything drastic suddenly like cutting all ties with people with low ratings. Just become aware of the 'quality' of the relationship and whether you want to increase or decrease the time you spend with them.

Connections

Loneliness is increasingly a serious problem in our society. Even in a large city like London and Tokyo where the density of the population is much higher than other areas and the place is bustling with people and streets lit with colourful and bright lights, there are people suffering from loneliness.

This epidemic is not only among the ageing population, many young and middle-aged are also leading their lives disconnected and unable to form or sustain meaningful and loving friendships.

This could be because either we have forgotten how to connect with people or are too busy to keep connections alive. Sometimes people are only interested in what they gain from connections. Especially in business and professional environment, I notice some people are interested in getting to know someone only if they see the 'benefits' or the person as a potential customer or business partner.

People are generally busy, so having to manage social and business engagements have become another one of regular jobs.

But I want to talk about something deeper than just organising a social lunch or family get together. Because the deep connection is essential to life, just like food and water.

Doctors are warning that loneliness is more devastating to

health than obesity and lonely people are nearly twice as likely to die prematurely than those who are not suffering from isolation.

Can you imagine spending your life building a business empire and living in a massive mansion and find yourself alone later in life because you never made a meaningful connection with people?

If you think it will happen to you, then look around, there may be people around you who could do with a little care and attention.

If you are genuinely interested in people and connect with people with good vibes, you will be able to form better relationships with people that can bring joy to all, and exchange positive energy. Deep and lasting connections begins with being authentic and listening with empathy where you leave your external persona behind and share your true self.

Creating time to connect is vital to your health and wellbeing.

Pace - Time Is a Valuable Commodity

The people who have visited Japan and took public transport know that Japanese society expects the service to run according to the timetable. Train platforms have markings to show where the doors on the train will and are expected to stop and its doors to open so that people can make an orderly queue while they wait. People expect the train and buses to arrive on time, not earlier, not later. That is how the Japanese people have got used to planning the journey in the most time-efficient manner.

No matter how wealthy you are, time is not something you can buy. Of course, with money, you will have more options on how you spend your time, but there will always be only 24 hours in a day. The length of time you have on this earth is also not something you can control. None of us knows exactly how long we have.

Time cannot be stopped or rewound. We cannot hold on to the moment or go back in time to re-experience it. Everything that is happening now in your life and what happens tomorrow will soon be in the past; only to be recalled in your memory.

Things that will determine your future is the decisions and actions you take today. If what you do today affects the outcome of your future, how important is it to do the things today that is more likely to bring the outcome you want in the future?

If you have already set goals and target for future dates. You might have a vision board full of photos of stuff you desire to have pasted on it.

But don't sit there and dream of the day that those visions will come true just by meditating. It is time to get up and make it happen. This is when the real creativity comes in.

Take a look at how you spend your time at the moment. Are you using your precious time in the most effective way? Using your time effectively does not mean you need to be productive constantly. Spending time to rejuvenate your body mind and soul is as important, and you need to allocate plenty of time to do this. This may take in various forms of having fun with your loved ones, playing with your kids, watching a movie, relaxing in the sun or sleeping. Whatever way you choose to rejuvenate yourself, make sure you are rejuvenating, not getting more stressed or worrying about other things.

Your time should be split into either restoring yourself or being productive but nothing in between. If you are having a nice dinner with your date but your mind is focused on your business plan, you are neither being productive nor being restorative.

Get the difference?

If you are trying to get to sleep but financial worry keeps you awake, that is not using the time for rejuvenation.

Sometimes, when your precious time is taken up by meeting, talking, associating or texting or chatting to people you may not consciously register it a waste of time. Consider whether those activities are having a positive effect on you. Be almighty aware of how you spend your time. Be either productive or restorative but nothing in between.

Do not waste your time just drifting, idling or waiting for something to happen. Engage with people, provide value, help others, educate your children, learn new things and keep growing.

So, when you get to the ripe old age of something, you do not look back and say to yourself, I wish I had done…. It would be so devastating that you have wasted your time that you will never get back.

Creating Time Creatively

How often do you say to yourself, 'I just haven't the time to do…'?

As I promised; this book is about implementing practical aspects of zen philosophy and therefore I don't expect you to need to take time off to do something special such as going on a zen retreat which you keep meaning to do but haven't the time to do.

Instead, I would like you to think about a time when you managed to fit an activity between your busy schedule because it was important to you.

This could be a music concert on a weekday night even though you needed to get up early the next day for work. Other times, it might have been scheduling three meetings back to back because you needed to finish work at a certain time to be able to get to your child's football match.

So, if something is important enough, you create time for it and you fit it in. If there are things you have always wanted to do but you think it is because you never had the time to do those, is simply because they were not important enough for you.

If you change your mindset to knowing that you are in control of how you spend your time and you can create the time of what is important to you, you will no longer use a sentence that begins with 'I don't have the time'. Because you actually do have as much time as you want as long as they are important enough for you to make it a priority.

Knowing this fact that you can create time, think about the things you have been putting off doing and how important they are for you.

What have you been saying you haven't the time to do lately; time to re-connect with old friends? time to start a business? time to play?

If you have been blaming 'lack of time' for not getting around to transforming your life for the better, change your language and stop yourself next time you come up with this excuse.

I remember my house has always been a lot cleaner and tidier when I was busy working than when I was a stay at home mum. When I was at home every day, I kept putting doing the cleaning off because I could do it anytime in the week, so the cleaning task got postponed often. You could say I procrastinated about cleaning the house. But when I was busy working five days a week, I had just a few hours on Saturday morning to get the cleaning done, before other activities that were crammed into each weekend took over, so I did it.

A task will take as long as the time you allow for it. When you give yourself a deadline on doing something, you are more likely to achieve your goal.

You can create time; it is down to you to decide how valuable it is for you.

Make a list of things you have been wanting to do but you have been thinking you have not had time to tackle. Don't do it later when you think you have time. Get yourself a notebook or something you won't throw away and write the list now.

It could be things like, decide on your investment options, inviting friends for dinner or clearing that dead tree in the garden. Whatever it is that have been in your mind to do in the last 12 months or so, include in the list.

Then number the list by order of importance and urgency regardless of whether you enjoy the task or not. For example, you have been unhappy with your current work but you think you have not had the time to do anything about it because you are always exhausted, but doing this task will improve your mental health, bring more money and improve harmony in your family because you will be happier and able to remember that life can be fun, then you might find something like this is treated as a top priority.

When you have numbered them all, rewrite the list on a new page from number 1 being at the top and give it a deadline; the exact date you will complete the task by. If you are overwhelmed by the enormity of the task, chunk it down to bite-size so monitor the progress each week. If it is a task that can be completed in a day or two; like visiting your grandma in the nursing home, pick a day of the visit now and schedule it in your diary before your mind comes up with other excuses why you can't.

If it is important enough for you, you will find the time.

Creating Business Through Harmony

Whenever I go to motivational seminars and workshops, we hear the speakers talk about how it is possible to reach whatever your goals are and the only thing stopping success from happening is yourself.

In the personal development scene, we all believe that what you desire is on the other side of fear or we have to break barriers of self-doubt and limiting beliefs.

I have listened to these many times and I too preach this to all, including family members and friends.

But I also know that just by knowing this fact does not exactly help change things dramatically.

The idea of creating what you desire by using the power of thought is not exactly a new idea. It's been talked about by Napoleon Hill in Think and Grow Rich, by Wallace Waddle in the Science of Getting Rich, The Strangest Secret by Earl Nightingale, and then The Secret by Rhonda Byron.

At first, you might think it is like magic.

Since the internet-based business has been booming and many people have been able to create a wealth of huge scale in a business model which did not exist before, you could say that power of the internet is the only source of such success which is a kind of magic.

Online affiliate marketing is one of them. Although a referral programme has always existed in the past whereby one earns a commission or a percentage of the value of a sale by referring a customer or making a sale, the internet has made it a lot easier.

Whatever you decide to do, it should be something you feel passionate about. I made a mistake of choosing a business because my main focus was to make money. And I wanted to make money as easily as possible at the time. Especially back then as a single mother and an over-worked salaried accountant, it was in my nature to calculate the profitability and the break-even point on any new ideas.

But as a result, that actually prevented me from getting started on a project. I also found that 100% of my heart was not in the business I was trying to grow.

It was a bit like an artist deciding on what to create based on the profitability of the end product. It is not possible. When you are dealing with passion and authenticity, you cannot always put a price tag on it before it happens. But I don't recommend going into business just based on passion. A suitable business model is essential.

A painting of an artist is valued at the price someone is prepared to pay. It is not something you can estimate or guess. Is that bad as a business model?

If so, consider this, selling something that you already know has a market value, such as generic products and services, that other people are already selling. For example, you saw fidget spinners are trending so you think it is a safe bet.

If your business sells exactly the same product as those already sold on the market, the profitability is dictated by the market. You then are restricted to the reality of the market share or a minimum number of products you have to sell in order to make a profit. You then get into the trap of focusing on the numbers rather than the problem you are trying to solve for the customers through your product.

The key is not to focus on the money but to focus on the value you want to provide to the world and the solution to problems you want to solve.

As soon as I stopped focusing on the amount of money I wanted to be earning, money started coming to me. This is because I adjusted my energy frequency to that of universal intelligence.

Be in business to solve real problems for people. To make their lives better, bring joy and make the world a better place. When you have helped people, then you create positive emotions, for them as well as in yourself. Positive emotions affect how you conduct your business, how you relate to others that you work with and your customers.

Instead of thinking about taking something from people or other businesses such as money and advice, focus on giving value and solving problems. Even if you don't think it will manifest directly into profit or something beneficial to you what you are doing is creating positive emotions that can encourage positive energy to flow towards you more and more each day.

HOW YOU GROW

"Do not dwell in the past, do not dream of the future, concentrate the mind on the present moment."

-Buddha

Your Personal Development Journey

The problem with talking about enlightenment and spiritual growth is that it is seen as an 'alternative' or 'new age'. Some people think such an idea has no place in business or wealth building.

I suppose I had the same problem.

For years, I could not see the parallels between enlightenment and profit-producing business activities.

My interest in spiritual growth and personal development started in my early twenties around the same time I was trying to build a business.

But the more I sought inner peace and harmony, the further I got from my business to thrive. It could be because, in those days, I was mixing with spiritual people who were far from being wealthy. They were making an okay living, talking about being 'one with nature' and promoting universal harmony.

Once you experience this 'oneness' you know that is the gateway to enlightenment. They were spiritually aware, into natural remedies and promoting universal harmony. They were kind and loving people but were not exactly living the dream.

The problem was I always felt there was a conflict within myself for wanting to sustain that state of being and wanting to attract wealth. I wanted to be successful. I didn't want to live a life of scarcity. I thought I had to choose one or the other.

When the idea of the law of attraction came about through the book of The Secret, we realised that it was not a secret at all. We knew all along how the universe worked. But a lot of us did not ask for wealth to come to us. Because we felt it was a self-centred act.

So, the conflict remained between wanting success and wanting enlightenment.

That is because we have lived with a mindset that wanting money equalled being greedy. This then naturally became my own limiting belief. As soon as I made some money, I either lost it by doing something silly with it or spent it so that I was back in the same place. Being poor. Because I believed albeit subconsciously, that being selfless and poor, I would attain enlightenment.

This vicious circle continued.

For many years, I listened to wealthy people talk, read books on creating wealth and did all the affirmations that they said I needed to do on a daily basis to attract wealth.

I signed up on many courses which promised to show exactly how they became extremely wealthy in a matter of months.

'Wow, that must be what I need to be doing', I thought.

'Yes, making some investment into this course is okay because I am going to get it back many times more when I am rich anyway'. Because all the business gurus say you have to invest in yourself etc.

So, the internal dialogue went on.

It was just another case of Shiny Object Syndrome.

It is also called SOS that many entrepreneurs suffer. You see a promise of your dream coming true, the people selling the program or tools tell you that it took them years to learn this but now they are going to share exactly how you can do the same by buying this information at an attractive price.

In other words, a promise of a shortcut to success.

Then you think, 'yeah, if I buy this, I will get there much more quickly, and I will be living my dream life just like this person selling the course in a matter of months if not weeks'. Because you think that you are buying a formula that gets you to where you want to be. A formula you think that works just like a mathematical equation or following a recipe. You get all the ingredients of success by buying this course and 'voila', there should be the end result, of you being rich beyond your dreams.

I have been there too.

But do you know what?

It did not happen to me. I spent the money, followed the course, took actions and waited for the result.

But the result was nothing extraordinary.

And I know this is not a unique story. This is the same story for the majority of people who buy those promises and supposedly a formula for success. In fact, it is as many as 95% who don't see any change in their life according to studies.

I had to go back to researching my soul and sought wisdom for the answer.

The answer I got was obvious.

Of course!

Why didn't I think of that?

I knew it all along. I just had been ignoring that message. How foolish of me. The answer was there all the time. I just didn't notice it.

It's a bit like when you are sitting by the roadside watching cars go by. You have been counting how many blue cars are driving past because you thought that was the answer to your problem. While doing that you had not taken any notice of the red cars at all. But there sure were many red cars went by. You just were not taking any notice of it. Because you had been focusing on the wrong colour!

A similar thing happens with romantic relationships. You

wonder why you have not had much luck with relationships over the years. And you come to realise you have been attracted to the totally wrong type of people. When you finally meet the right person, you might realise actually this person is not that unique. This person is not a superhuman who is rare and hard to find. You find that this type of person had always been around. It's just you had not been noticing them as a possible romantic partner. In other words, your frequency was different.

Anyway, that's another story.

So back to the red cars.

What I discovered; I had known all along. But I had not taken it seriously as the answer to my problems.

What I realised was I thought I bought a formula to be my solution. I tried to resolve my problem with training courses and intake of information.

But the reality was that it was not that 'thing' I bought that was missing from my life.

The missing ingredient was me! I was out of tune. I was

focusing on outcomes. I was not growing.

That is when the wisdom kicked in and taught me this.

When I have proved the value of my service only then I will receive the value in return. And that value must not be for my own personal gain. It must be in the best interest of all concerned. In other words, the energy I create must be of the highest frequency I am able to vibrate at, which will, in turn, encourage others to rise up, swim to and get on my boat. If I give them the ride on my boat, I can also help them get to where they want to go. Because we are all part of one giant network. We are all interconnected on the molecular level. What we do to that network, we do to ourselves.

Do you know what? Things started to change in my business and my life from that moment. Within days, my mind which was on par with 'I am poor and I can't afford stuff' changed to a higher frequency of 'I can manifest an abundant life'. Until that point, I had been working in a supermarket to make ends meet but within days, I got a new client who signed up for a 6 months contract with me which allowed me to leave the supermarket job and start working for myself.

I recently watched a webinar of someone who claims themselves as an abundance coach who was selling her own course. Everything she was saying about channelling the energy in the right way to attract abundant wealth was right. When she said changing your energy frequency to receive abundance from the universe, I resonated totally because that is what I believe how the universe works.

But I also know that it is not the act of buying this course that is going to make it happen.

It is only by learning how to realign yourself to the universe and tune into the energy that you will change something.

That will not happen automatically by just reading a book, attending a course or meditating for a couple of hours a day. Remember, Buddha, meditated for 49 days to receive enlightenment.

Not all of us have that much free time and we will soon get hungry or be compelled to check our phone for updates anyway.

It's just not practical.

That's why I work with people who want to work on themselves first to transform their life instead of looking for a simple formula. By going through this transformation process, and learning to adopt the way of SmartZen, it is usual to find your own 'thing' at the same time. A product, a service, an activity or whatever that is actually going to turn the value you give into the value you receive in return.

This value you receive in return might be more time, fulfilment, a sense of belonging, a passion or money, however, you define what success is. It will come to you more easily.

By changing your mindset and your belief system about wealth, success and happiness, that's when you will start seeing positive changes to your life.

Only by instilling this belief as your way of life on a daily basis that the transformation you are about to experience will become permanent.

You will notice that there more doors to more opportunities in front of you and you start attracting and meeting people who will take you higher with your own thing. You will discover that you had it in you all along. It just needed uncovering.

Therefore, it's called dis-covering of yourself.

This is vital to understand. You have heard about the 80/20 rule, right? It is also known as the Pareto Principle. This suggests that 20 per cent of your activities will account for 80 per cent of your results. What do you think is the vital 20% activity you should be doing right now?

Sustaining the SmartZen Mindset

As a dedicated personal development junkie, most of my life I have known the power of thoughts and how this can affect the outcome.

But nowadays there are so many materials that can motivate you and change your mindset from scarcity to abundance, from negative to positive that you can consume.

This is a sign of human evolution. Thirty years ago, when we had just come out of love and peace movement of the 60s and 70s, it was a revolution then, but the momentum had only been sustained by the minority.

But in recent years, the importance of being aware of our thoughts have been recognized in wider society. In the workplace and in many sports, it is more often now that individuals are evaluated and succeed by the mindset they hold rather than their technical ability.

In 2019, the importance of having the right mindset is acknowledged further and is becoming a common theme. Even schools are teaching children about developing grit, positive mindset and resilience to failures. We have come a long way.

But while 'you can get whatever you want in life if you put your mind to it' way of thinking has helped many people achieve the kind of extraordinarily exponential success; the majority of people are still living with the industrial way of thinking. They're still being led by others and are avoiding taking ownership of their own destiny.

Most people can agree with what we say about the power of thoughts is true. But they do not apply it to their own life, because they do not believe in it 100%. Perhaps they believe up to about 80%. The remaining 20% is what they consider to be the stuff that they have no control over that they think someone else controls somehow. They believe that the elements of their lives are controlled by external forces.

Things like when your partner behaved in such a way that made you feel angry or the government are making a terrible shamble with your country's economic future or even simple things like a sudden torrential rain and wind when you were just about to start filming your vlog. People can get caught up in a drama of it all just so that you can say, 'See? This law of attraction stuff doesn't work!'

As a result, you stop taking charge of your life because you go back to the mindset of, I am only in control of some part of my life. Or my thoughts are not strong enough or having the right mindset only works occasionally without realising that when you thought it hadn't happened is when you disconnected yourself from the universal force.

I had been in this push and pull relationship with the universal force for years…. actually, decades. I believed in the law of attraction and read Creative Visualisation or something similar again and got back to believing in the power of thoughts only to find myself a while later that I got defeated by the opposing thoughts like 'it doesn't actually work'.

The reason 90% of people are leading an average life, the top 10% hold 85% of world's wealth and half of the world's wealth is held by the 1% is probably because 90% of people don't believe in the power of thoughts 100% of the time.

Something else I have found that prevents most of us from fully applying the power of our thoughts to our life is what we actually think of ourselves deep down.

Most of us don't believe we deserve real happiness and success deep in our psyche.

Most probably because of the conditioning from your past as far back as your childhood. You may have experienced defeat one of another during the time you were still developing your ideas about what life is all about.

It could be that you didn't earn a medal for the 100m race at a school sports day or didn't get the grade you wanted for important exams.

It might be that you got rejected when you asked someone out on a date or at a job interview you had your high hopes on.

Gradually, we developed our way of thinking and our view of the world. Over the years, subconsciously we collected evidence of failures, defeats and disappointment. We made an assumption that top prizes always went to that able boy in the class or that girl I used to know who always got the best job in the field. We began to believe that a life of abundance and success happened to others and not to us.

This has led to our conclusion that we are not worthy of receiving what we desire.

This is despite developing our mindset as an adult and consciously thinking that this is not true. We are worthy.

But the conflict stays deep in our subconscious mind.

Even if as an adult you logically know that you are worthy of happiness, success and wealth, just like you believe, in fact, you have no doubt that your children are worthy of happiness, success and wealth. But you also know that you cannot simply buy your child all the toys he or she wants. You know, it is in their best interest not to have everything they ask for at Christmas and birthdays. Because you want them to learn that you don't get what you wish for simply by wishing and teach them about your work ethic or something similar. Most probably your parents would have done the same, all for your own good as responsible adults.

But in a child's mind, this restriction, this limit, this rule can easily develop into thinking that they do not deserve fun and joy all the time. Perhaps Christmas presents were a huge disappointment because they didn't get the latest toy they had wished for. Most of us grew up with similar experiences.

It is time to unravel the thoughts we learned back then. Thank our parents for keeping us on track, keeping away from trouble and teaching us self-discipline and delayed gratification.

It is now our turn to be a good parent for ourselves and reassure ourselves that it is okay because we are responsible enough to know what to do with all the fortunes, success and happiness the universe is going to give us. We can handle it.

In our society, being the most positive-minded individual in the sea of 100 people in your circle, in your community or an organisation might feel like swimming against the tide. It's like being in a room of 100 people and you will find 90 of them might never turn their life around.

But you will find 9 other like-minded people you might cling together to move forward. Those will might want to swim together because they also want an extraordinary life. There are plenty.

What I want to point out is that I have found you don't have to swim against the tide at all.

For example, if you focus on becoming the top 10% of the

wealthiest people through your mindset work and wealth creation method, sure you might get there eventually. But have you asked what you have done towards your own work to encourage wider wealth distribution?

If you are in a business to sell a gadget to as many people as possible meanwhile you had them manufactured in a sweatshop full of children in undeveloped country and contaminated the ocean with waste and chemicals while you got really rich yourself so that you can send your kids to private school and live your life on a white sandy beach, I would like you to think again what true wealth is about.

I would like you to think about creating wealth beyond your own life and immediate family, friends and community.

You don't have to take anything from them. There is plenty for all. Create a business that helps create wealth and success to customers and people you work with. Remember we are all made of the same stuff. We are part of the bigger network. If we harm a part of that network, we ultimately harm ourselves.

We must move away from the 'us and them' mindset we are all in the same sea trying to swim towards growth. Whatever you are selling to your customers, are you helping the humanity and ecology that exist on this planet?

Some rich people are planning to escape the earth by buying their way out to mars or other places where there is still a hope of enough food, clean water and air. Is that what you are aiming to do as well when you get super-rich?

What are we leaving for our children and their children and their children? It is time to shift a gear up and really change something radical with the wealth and richness you plan to create.

I said to my mentor the other day when I happened to attend a seminar he was running in London, how I understood what he had been telling us all along, which was not to chase money.

The money will come as a result of giving out value. I have found it to be so true.

When you start focusing on your own frequency to the universal energy and become consciously aware of your alignment to it, you will become so in tuned that you know whether you are on the right track or not immediately.

If your intentions are in line with the intention of the universe which is to expand and grow like all living things are meant to do, you will be able to create wealth more easily.

As I mentioned earlier, we live in a digital world where people are sharing their intimate details about their lifestyles. We can look into their lives visually and draw our opinions on what we think about them.

Sometimes we come across people who inspire us and lift us up to places perhaps each day or each week as if they hold your hand to help you navigate through the tough terrain of social drama, obstacles and negative energy.

These people used to be called leaders but nowadays you may call them influencers. Indeed, they influence us. They influence our views, our thinking and even our desires. Some of those people create 'wants' within our psyche by sharing their successes, their wealth and their achievements. It is all well and good if what you get from these influencers is a positive push you need and you feel inspired to be the best that you can be.

But there is a danger that these wants are not necessarily our personal 'wants'. When you see someone posting on social media sharing their affluent lifestyle, how do you feel? Do you feel you want that for yourself? Do you feel that you are missing out on things that you could be having?

Then you might start researching how they made their fortune and get into the way of thinking that you should be doing the same. believing that is the missing link in your life that you had been looking for.

Stop yourself from being outward-looking. We are in a way all searching for answers to the many questions we have. We know that if our goal is to earn twice as much this year and when we reach it, we want more next year. When we see our friends with the latest gadgets, we want one of those, too.

Stop looking for answers outside and start looking inwards.

When we were born, we came into the world with nothing. When we die, we will not be taking anything with us other than the memories we shared.

If you think you are working hard to collect items to leave behind for your children, think again. When our mother and father pass away, do you think of them by the material things that they left for us? Rather than the heirloom, they leave for us, it is the memory that you shared together that actually outlasts any of materials things, regardless of whether the memories are good or bad.

In many ways, it is a great burden for the loved ones left behind to tidy up the material stuff afterwards. The greatest gift you can leave is your love and the wonderful memories you create.

That is the most important legacy you can also leave to the people you leave behind.

I do not deny the fact that collecting assets have always been one of the things to do when the future was uncertain. We will talk about building wealth in the next section. But the greatest assets we can build for our life and the loved ones is really is our healthy mind and body for as long as possible so that you feel at peace with yourself, connect with loved ones and to spread happiness to others.

So, what can we do when we are constantly bombarded with external stimulation that influences us to a greater or lesser degree?

We need to look inwards to reconsider what we really believe to be a successful life. It doesn't matter what other people are getting up to. It doesn't matter what other people are accomplishing or not accomplishing. Stop judging others and start evaluating your own state of being.

We are constantly being fed ideas of the alternatives; what we could be doing, what we could be having, what we could be buying.

When we listen, read or watch stuff, we are cluttering our brain. You should be feeding your brain with information that empowers us for growth and well-being.

Instead of asking 'I wonder what that celebrity is up to', change your question to 'what can I be doing that can impact our world in a positive way'?

Instead of thinking, 'what else can I buy next?', ask yourself 'how can I use this money to enhance experiences of our existence?'.

When you wonder why I don't have what so and so have in material wealth, change your thinking to expressing your gratitude for what you already have.

If your mind has held a belief that your background, lack of something, inadequacy or even the society has brought you to where you are, you have to start remembering that you are creating your own perspective with the mindset you have been holding. When you let go of the belief that you are controlled by some external forces that put you in the current place, you will begin to shift your place in the world.

Because the truth is when you change your perspective and vibrate at high frequency, you will be able to respond better to whatever life presents.

Accept the presence of your own negative thoughts but choose to hold the thoughts that open the pathway to success, happiness, love and health.

It is about spring cleaning your mindset and growing spiritually.

Redefining Wealth

When you have cleansed your body and mind, declutter your home and social network, reevaluated what success really looks like for you and recognized the preciousness of time, you return to the fundamental place where you can start to see clearly what life is all about.

Although we are all meant to reach our own full potential and live an abundant life, you will begin to realise that breaking your back and compromising your well-being to achieve success or becoming rich by sacrificing other people and the planet is no longer an option you are willing to entertain.

We have explored how our external forces continue to influence how we form our opinions on success and wealth. You know that you do not need to lead a life of excessive material-gathering or achieve a certain status to be really happy.

I have also talked about how success is created by being happy and being content first.

But when it comes to wealth building, we also have mixed feelings about this.

You may have heard a fable about a fisherman and an American businessman in the past. Here is one version of that story.

The Fisherman and the Businessman

An American businessman was at the pier of a small coastal village when a small boat with just one fisherman docked. Inside the small boat were several large yellowfin tunas. The businessman complimented the fisherman on the quality of his fish and asked how long it took to catch them.

The fisherman replied, "only a little while."

The businessman then asked why didn't he stay out longer and catch more fish?

The fisherman said he had enough to support his family's immediate needs.

The businessman then asked, "but what do you do with the rest of your time?"

The fisherman said, "I sleep late, fish a little, play with my children, take naps with my wife, and stroll into the village each evening where I sip wine and play in the band with my friends. I have a full and busy life."

The businessman scoffed. "I have an MBA from Harvard, and can help you," he said. "You should spend more time fishing, and with the proceeds, buy a bigger boat. With the proceeds from the bigger boat, you could buy several boats, and eventually, you would have a fleet of fishing boats. Instead of selling your catch to a middle-man, you could sell directly to the top Japanese restaurants in town, eventually opening up your own fresh tuna sashimi business.

You could control the product, processing, and distribution," he said. "Of course, you would need to leave this small coastal fishing village and move to a city, then Los Angeles, and eventually to New York City, where you will run your expanding enterprise."

The fisherman asked, "But, how long will this all take?"

To which the businessman replied, "Oh, 15 to 20 years or so."

"But what then?" asked the fisherman.

The businessman laughed and said, "That's the best part. When the time was right, you would announce an IPO, and sell your company stock to the public and become very rich. You would make millions!"

"Millions – then what?"

The businessman said, "Then you could retire. Move to a small coastal fishing village where you could sleep late, fish a little, play with your kids, take naps with your wife, and stroll to the village in the evenings where you could sip wine and play in the band with your friends..."

This is the sort of story, most of us play in our head and experience some kind of moral dilemma. Because you could be someone like the American businessman as well as the Fisherman.

While there might be a clear moral to the story, what the American businessman is describing could equally be regarded as natural progress, pursuing a life of abundance and success of the enterprise that can contribute to the economy of the country and create jobs for people. But I'm sure you also agree that the fisherman man is already living a life of plenty. He has the freedom to sleep late, plenty of food, time to play with his kids, relaxed enough to take a nap with his wife in the afternoon and enjoy the active social life.

This is where some of us who pursue the path to enlightenment, inner peace and happiness might conclude that you don't want the huge enterprise that the American businessman is suggesting because ultimately you already have what you desire here and now.

Because most of us believe that we cannot have both happiness and wealth.

Before exploring ways to have both wealth and happiness, let me ask you this. When you think about success and wealth, does your mind immediately go to thinking it is about having a large house, a boat, a jet and a few sports cars, luxury brand handbags and more? If so, you are simply suffering from material FOMO.

With digital technology, it is easier to have a peek on the private lives of super-rich and follow them as they showcase their material wealth. They probably worked very hard to get those and no one can deny it is a great achievement.

But you define being wealthy is simply to gather material items, I would like you to stop and think there. The research shows that material wealth does not bring you lasting happiness or a sense of fulfilment in the way that you might imagine.

You might be excited and happy when you have bought something new especially something you have wanted for a while. The sense of fulfilment is there. You would think such joy would last as long as the item exists. Material things can create moments of positive emotions of joy and happiness. But the majority of cases, your happiness is short-lived.

If someone asks you what the happiest moment in the last 12 months was that you could remember, it would most probably be about an experience of time spent in some way, perhaps with friends or loved ones. Even if it is related to an accomplishment it is more to do with the moment and the experience of it, rather than about obtaining a material item. It is through experience that we are more likely to feel happiness.

So why are we at times obsessed with buying more material stuff when we already have enough and what we have are in perfectly good condition? I once read about interesting research into how materialism is connected to low self-esteem. In the study, children were shown a number of different images and asked to choose images of things that make them happy. They found that children who chose material things such as toys and games were generally found to be low in self-esteem in comparison to children who chose experiences such as friendships and learning a new musical instrument as a source of happiness. The research found a strong link with materialism with low self-esteem in children.

You can imagine what kind of adult those children might grow up to be and where they eventually look for happiness. Materialism in adults might therefore also be related to low self-esteem in the same way. That should not come as a great surprise. We are constantly bombarded with images and ideas from advertisements that try to make us believe we need those things to feel good about ourselves. The advertisers can poke the part of our brain that already feels inadequate in some way to make us believe that it could be remedied with another new material item added to our already cluttered lives.

Just like the fisherman in the story, it is not through material wealth that we will find happiness or true wealth. It is rather contrary. Oftentimes, it is the simple thing such as a moment of realisation that you already have everything you need. It could be the afternoon you spent with our children laughing or woke up to see the sunrise over a mountain or at a fun gathering with friends you love. It may also be time spent helping others in some way through volunteering. It could be through giving others an opportunity to flourish in their own way.

Everyone is worthy of living an abundant life. I highly respect people who have succeeded financially. Some of those people are the most loving and generous people I have ever met who also help others achieve equally successful lives. There is nothing wrong with pursuing a successful business enterprise and financial freedom.

So, if such moments and experience of bliss are what you desire and where happiness is found, you need freedom of time to do this. You need to be able to choose how you spend your precious time. In order to achieve this, you will most probably need money. Because money is what our society uses to exchange and allow you to achieve freedom of time. As I said earlier, money is a tool and it is what buys hospitals, schools, fuel for warmth and food for the family.

The idea of building wealth is basically to create time and freedom in which you can lead more harmonious life which is in line with your true purpose and mission. If you build wealth, you are in a better position to sustain the mindset of abundance. Then any surplus you create can be used to help others. Instead of gathering material goods, if you build wealth through careful planning, business building and investments, you will continue to create a life in which you have more freedom of choice on not only how you live but how you serve the society and this planet.

So, the dilemma is not whether to pursue wealth like the American businessman or happiness like the fisherman.

You don't need to choose either. The dilemma is how you can build wealth and what you will do with it.

Why not build a lifestyle that allows you to be happy and content and look for ways to create wealth so that you can continue to lead the lifestyle you want as well as help others and the planet you cherish. Remember, we are made of the same stuff, we are all connected in the interconnected network.

If you build wealth from the perspective of abundant wealth

for all, and not through the mindset of depriving of wealth and richness from others, you will build wealth through awaken state of being and in harmony with the universal force.

Become super-rich if that is what your goal is but think about what you would do with your wealth and your position. Think carefully how you would impact others and the planet during and after your enterprise building. Consider how you can expand your enterprise to make a real difference. Not because you want to live your life of excess.

"Success is liking yourself, liking what you do, and liking how you do it."

- Maya Angelou

Moving Meditation as a Routine

We often talk about living in the present but do we know what it really means?

We also hear people say, live every day as it is your last.

If I was to take this advice literally, I would go and do

something thinking this is my last chance and I would probably do something outrageous and end up regretting it because I HAVE to live with the consequences.

So, this advice is not that useful.

We talked about setting goals for the future earlier in this book. Knowing your destination helps to determine what you should be doing now to reach your goals.

But we must not forget about staying in the present moment to appreciate the life we currently lead.

Life is not perfect; at times it is chaotic and stressful. But it is because of those moments we experience that life has its meaning. Without negative experiences, we cannot recognise the positive. We cannot deny the existence of darkness to see the light.

Because everything in life comes a pair of opposites. One cannot exist without the other, just like there are two sides to a coin.

Whenever we try to deny what we don't want from life we do not create a room for what we want. The same can be said for our own psyche. If we deny that we do also possess the dark side to our personality, we cannot become the person we wish to be.

Unless we recognise that we occasionally experience the darkest emotion of hatred, greed, selfishness, maleficient nature of our core being at times strong enough to murder someone for our own protection, we cannot be in control of our emotion enough to choose our alternative behaviour. When you have recognised that you have this dark side within you, you are in a safe place to be yourself.

Because to maintain the right balance in your psyche, you cannot just pick to hold thoughts on the nice bits about yourself. You also have to recognise that you can be a self-centred, an annoying brat, a lazy sod and an anti-social recluse. When you have accepted that part of yourself, you are empowered to choose your behaviour and how you conduct yourself every day. And therefore, you can maintain the right balance between the light and the dark.

We will talk about this way of thinking in the final section of this book.

For now, you can go with the idea that a regular personal reflection is needed to maintain your balance.

It doesn't mean you have to sit in silence to do this. In ancient Japan, part of the teaching of Zen was not meditating in silence but through tea ceremonies and ikebana or kadō, the Japanese flower arrangement or shodo, calligraphy.

Much of Japanese ceremony derived from spiritual practice and tea ceremony, as an example, was actively practised by Buddhists in the 15th Century. Its form has not changed much and the ceremony is less to do with a tasting of the tea, but rather, its principles lies in harmony, respect, purity and tranquillity.

Zen calligraphy, practised by **Buddhist** monks and also by people in general in Japan from primary school children is also a type of ceremony in itself.

When we talk about calligraphy in the west it is often the end result of what it is created that has the importance. But with Zen calligraphy, it is the process of 'writing' itself that has the meaning. One is encouraged to clear one's mind and let one's hand flow itself. It is the movement of energy that translates into letters on the paper. It stresses the connection between your body and the universal energy that we talked about earlier.

The Japanese tea ceremony is called chadō, and calligraphy is called shodō, the flower arrangement is called kadō. Most of the Japanese martial art form also ends with the word dō, such as aikidō, bushidō, kendō and judō.

The word 'dō' means a way or a path.

Like the practice of Yoga, through the movement of your body, you attain the harmony between your body and mind and re-calibrate your frequency of vibration to the universal energy. This can be done when you are arranging flowers, writing, drawing or even making tea, in fact carrying out any of your daily activities from simple tasks such as cutting vegetables, walking your dog, folding clothes or washing your body.

This practice of being aware of your connection to the universal energy, the status of your being, once becomes a habit, will be like an oasis you return to many times of the day.

When it becomes a norm to be in that state, you will start feeling uncomfortable if you are not being connected to the universal energy or being in the harmonious state in body and mind.

There are many other ways you can do moving meditation. Perhaps walking through the forest, or sitting by a beach, lying on a grass gazing at the sky. There are endless ways to feel in your body and mind that you are a part of a bigger force, a bigger network of interconnected energy and all you need to do is learn to tune in, realign yourself as often as possible.

Tuning Into The Universal Energy

I don't think I need to tell you how the thoughts you hold can affect your life and the outcome.

Not only from the vast amount of information available nowadays to prove the power of thoughts, but we are also familiar with self-fulfilling prophecies where beliefs can manifest reality. This can be positive or negative.

SmartZen is based on this belief and by following this book, you have been learning how to create a right physical and mental environment for the manifestation of beliefs to occur more easily, effortlessly and quickly.

I hope you understand that by recognising how our lives are a part of a large interconnected network of energy, we have to look at our life as a whole in order to improve the results.

Whatever it is, if you believe, it is manifested. Whether it is good or bad, the universe does not care, it will give you what you believe.

If you believe life is bad, you will be subconsciously channelling negative energy and the universe will respond accordingly.

On the other hand, if you believe that you can manifest good health, an abundance of success and happiness for all concerned, you will channel that energy by raising your frequency to connect with the universe. And the universe will also respond accordingly.

Learning to tune into universal energy is the way to create this channel.

As I discussed earlier, you do not have to be sitting still to connect yourself to the universal energy. But until you can synchronise with that energy easily without effort, you may want to practice in a quiet place.

You may sit in a chair or lie down and close your eyes.

Start focusing on your breathing and notice your lungs expand as they fill up with air and as you breath out how your chest shrinks. Repeat this several times all the time you are focusing on your breaths.

Then continue breathing, but as you breathe out, notice the areas where the surface of your body touches the chair or the bed. It might be your bottom and your back and notice the pressure your body is feeling on the surface. I want you to remember that the molecules in your body are made of the same fundamental atoms that your chair or the bed is made of.

Start slowing your breathing down. In total relaxation, you do not need to breathe rapidly. As your body slows down you may feel your heart from inside of your body. Each time you breathe out, notice that your body's surface sinks into the surface of your bed or the chair as the vibration of your body begins to match with the vibration of the chair or the bed.

When your vibration is in tune with that surface you will start to notice that there is no longer the distinction between your body and the chair.

Now feel the vibration of the whole of your body synchronises with the frequency of the universal energy. You may even feel the sensation that the surface of your body is no longer distinct from the air in the room. You are blending into the universal network.

When you have reached this stage, you will know instinctively. This is how you can manifest your beliefs by channelling the energy in the right way.

Use this moment to feel gratitude for the life you have. Feel the love all around you; take stock of how it makes you feel and be grateful. Express gratitude for love, for food, for shelter and for all the things you might have taken for granted until now including your health and wellbeing.

Be appreciative of the lessons you have learnt particularly the hard lessons. It is those experiences that can make you wiser and stronger now. Try to look within for the feeling of compassion towards the people who have upset you or made you angry. Especially for those who caused an event that still disturbs your inner peace today: forgive them and let them go.

Be thankful for the life you are about to lead which may be in line with the success you set earlier in this book.

Finally, feel the happiness that fills your whole body that assures you that everything you believe to be good and right is with you already and you believe in the universal energy.

Practice this as often as possible until it becomes your default setting and a state you hold each day. You will learn more from me in the SmartZen programs.

HOW YOU IMPACT

"To follow the path, look to the master, follow the master, walk with the master, see through the master, become the master. "
– Zen Proverb

Educating The Future Generation

The department of education in the UK announced that it aimed to introduce mindfulness and meditation technique in schools as part of one of the largest studies in the world. The study will last until 2021 involving children from 370 schools in England. They will test the different approaches to support and improve children's mental health.

As a mother and a grandmother, I celebrate this move by the government in principle. I have always felt that we have been too slow to recognise the importance of mental health in children. We are too quick to try to eliminate the symptoms of illness or disorder rather than investigate the real cause, which might lie within the psyche. We have relied upon medications to suppress the discomfort instead of exploring the root cause itself. We have been only looking at the individual ailments and for individual solutions rather than looking at the child's body and the mind or the environment such as close family as a whole.

Having said this, I worry that the government's plan to test the effectiveness of various methods to improve children's mental health is simply another way to test which methods eliminate the symptoms the best. If so, they are missing the whole point.

Of course, making meditation as part of the daily practice helps everyone. That is why adults have taken up the habit by millions in recent years. Even large corporations see the benefits of encouraging their employees to have these quiet times to themselves while at work.

Studies have shown the health benefits of meditation include reduced blood pressure, easing the symptoms of anxiety and depression in employees as well as improvements in employee engagement, focus and performance.

But mindfulness or meditation or whatever you want to call it, it is basically a practice of self-awareness. Long ago, perhaps before the technologies have transformed our lives, self-awareness was not a luxury. It had been practised by a few wise people.

I come from a county where self-awareness is instilled from an early age. I would not for a moment claim that Japan does not have its own social problems. In Japan like any other developed countries, have issues with bullying in schools and suicides of young people.

But there are things Japanese people do very differently and I believe that it plays an important part in developing children's lives in becoming well-adjusted members of society. Many people describe Japanese people as 'polite'. Perhaps in English, that is the only word that can describe the way Japanese people conduct themselves.

I would describe this 'politeness' to stem from being self-aware.

In Japan, it normally starts from a very early age and it is formally practised in school from the early years of primary age group. The school is the ideal institution to model a society where children have to learn and work alongside other people. And that is where learning to be self-aware starts.

Just to introduce a couple of examples; it is a normal practice for all children to clean their own classroom at the end of each day before they go home. This usually involves moving the desks and chairs to one side, sweeping and wiping the floor. After cleaning, the cleaning team has to put all the desks and chairs back where they were, ready for the following day. They accept this duty as a norm.

In order for the collective cleaning to take place effectively, each child is responsible for putting their belongings away and keeping the area tidy. This gives an opportunity for each child in turn to clean the classroom. Through gentle peer pressure, they learn how their behaviour can become a burden to others by not tidying up their own belongings. Of course, they quickly learn how annoying it is if someone else does not clear up after themselves or skip their turn for the cleaning duty. If a child continues to annoy others, they might be disliked by other classmates and eventually experience isolation from the group and the network. The ultimate fear for anyone.

They don't just clean their own classrooms. Instead of having dinner ladies and gents as attendants, the children serve lunch for each other. Serving food for each other and tidy up after lunch together is a normal daily routine for all primary school children aged 7 to 12 in Japan.

This is not a government's attempt to save money on employing cleaning and school dinner staff. These small acts of daily routines are actually playing a much more important role in each child's development.

They teach self-awareness, teamwork skills, a sense of responsibility and compassion for others.

They teach how their own conduct affects others in the class and therefore in turn how it affects themselves as well. It is a different learning experience for the children from when adults simply telling them how to behave.

The children are learning how each other's behaviour causes each other to feel a certain way. They learn to put themselves in other people's shoes and they learn to adjust their own behaviour accordingly. Of course, similar learning can be arranged through academic lessons and physical education, but collective cleaning and serving others lunch teaches important social responsibility.

If they don't help with cleaning the classroom, it affects all the classmates as the classroom will be in a bad state the next morning. Or If they don't serve the lunch on time and finish clearing up afterwards, the playtime gets shorter. As a result, everyone knows what it is to be accountable.

This teaching makes them quite intuitive about how they play an important part in their school society as an individual. They experience that their contribution to that society is valued as much as they value other's contribution.

It seems simple but it is not hard to see how highly effective this arrangement could be and how it could influence how they grow up to become members of the larger society later on. It's a pity my own three children missed out on this experience by growing up in the UK.

We can recall the press reporting Japanese people's calm and resilience after the major earthquake and tsunami in 2011 when people were queueing patiently for hours for essentials instead of looting. Many people might remember more recent news highlighting Japanese people's 'politeness' after Japan's defeat against Belgium in the 2018 football World Cup. As if, it was a complete surprise when the tearful fans stayed behind to clear up the stadium and the defeated Japanese team left the locker room clean and tidy with a message of gratitude.

We should live in a society where that happens all the time, don't you think?

I remember visiting many schools in England as a prospective parent at different stages of my children's life. My visit included notable private schools where affluent families send their children to. They pay thousands of Pounds each term for their children to be educated there. Sometimes I was horrified to see the messy corridors with their belongings thrown on the floor. I could not see the correlation between their academic performance and the poor level of the student's conduct in basic areas such as taking care to keep the corridor free from hazards as a member of the school community.

Research shows that mental stability is related to calmness and resilience in times of stress. We know from studies that people who recognise their own value by being of service to others are far happier than people who simply donated money to charity. Recognising our own value is a part of having a healthy relationship with one's self. It is the foundation of a healthy relationship with others and therefore the wider world. It makes sense for this healthy relationship with ourselves to start early in life.

Do not make a mistake of thinking this is about sacrificing yourself for other people. This is not about putting others first before yourself. It is not about abnegation or denial of self-expression. Being self-aware keeps you grounded and at peace with yourself. Being self-aware is a 'skill' that should be learned not just for your own well-being but to support the well-being of others around you, the family, the community, and the society as a whole.

I believe we need to educate and support the new generation to be more self-aware and to promote their well-being created by being of service and value to each other.

How You Impact Through Business

I get it.

'We are in business to make money'.

That's the usual saying.

The main aim of a business is to make a profit. If you don't make a profit, it's called a charity.

But I think businesses need to start paying attention to the impact it has on people and the world beyond the office walls. That includes the well-being of their people.

When I was working for a corporate organisation, they were planning an office move to a larger office space to accommodate the growing number of employees. At the designing stage, I asked whether they were planning to incorporate a space for employees where they could sit and have a quiet moment. They quickly dismissed the idea with a little giggle. Needless to say, a quiet space where employees can meditate during lunchtime or sit quietly at a coffee break was as never provided.

The funny thing is they made sure there was an area outside, dedicated to smokers.

When you think about it, how does that make sense?

I got interested in finding out what other companies provided spaces for meditation or quiet spaces as part of a well-being enhancing provisions to employees.

What I find amazingly wonderful is that more companies are beginning to recognise the importance of helping employees to attain inner peace instead of continuously driving productivities in the workplace.

Some tech companies are providing rooms where employees can take a few minutes of downtime to zone out, relax, stretch, nap, or even meditate.

Research has found that meditation in the workplace can lower the number of absences due to sickness thereby reducing the costs to the company. Helping to boost employees' morale, mental focus and sense of well-being, thus increasing productivity anyway.

This is not surprising as we already know the health benefits of regular meditation in reducing blood pressure and stress thereby improving decision-making skills. Big companies like Apple, Nike, Google, Sony and Facebook seem to have embraced meditation space as part of their working life.

A wellness Institute of Cleveland Clinic has gone as far as to say that in their study, meditation not only lowers stress and increase employee engagement but also lead to happier employees.

Some research says that big businesses are being smart by reading the study of how balanced worker is more beneficial to their businesses. They do not consider the time employees spend mediating as a wasteful idle time, instead, they know it helps their staff to get things done. Those businesses know that creativity and focus come from the mental well-being of their workers.

The result of the study[*6] is astounding.

- 91 per cent reported it positively impacted the culture
- 88 per cent would recommend it to a co-worker
- 66 per cent said they felt less stress or had improved stress-management capabilities
- 63 per cent are better able to manage themselves at work
- 60 per cent reported increased focus and better decision-making skills

- 52 per cent are able to better manage work relationships
- 46 per cent reported increased innovation and creativity

Having said this, just because you have provided your employees with a space to chill out, it doesn't necessarily tackle the important issue of the working culture of the rat race. Again, we have to think about the cause of the stress and not stop at just treating the symptoms.

Even in the UK, it has been said that work-related stress costs the UK economy, nearly £6.5 million every year. The traditional working environment is creating employees who are not only struggling with stress, but they are disengaged, tired and unmotivated to work.

How depressing is that?

How About 4 Day A Week?

Is working 4 days a week a simpler way of resolving the imbalance?

While I welcome the idea of a 4-day week or long weekends as an idea for better work-life balance, I don't believe simply working four days a week instead of five is the answer.

From society's perspective, if we are going to rely on improving people's work-life balance by reducing the number of hours or days we work, I think we first need to look at how productivity is measured.

The idea of measuring work by hours with '8 hours a day' unit might have been suitable when measuring a worker's productivity at an assembling line in a factory, but it is an ancient idea.

Some Northern European counties work 6-hour-day without losing productivity or income. Is it coincident that those countries are consistently in the top ten happiest countries in the world?

There is also a problem that many organisations suffer from a type of employee described as 'coasters' who plod along each day doing the minimum work until it is time to go home. Isn't this because their salary is still being measured by the number of hours they work or stay in the office rather than their productivity level?

Isn't it better to pay those employees by how much work

they have actually carried out, meaning how much they have been productive, rather than how many hours they spent in the office?

There is also another angle with a work-life balance that we must not ignore. When you do something you truly enjoy, you do not feel there is an imbalance between work and life. Some people who lead their lives based on passion and purpose may work long hours without feeling tired or feeling deprived of freedom.

They are not usually the ones complaining about the lack of work-life balance.

The imbalance is felt in the mind and body of people who feel unmotivated, unfulfilled and unrewarded adequately for their efforts. When I say reward, I don't just mean money, but I also refer to intangible rewards such as gratitude and recognition.

We must recognise that the imbalance can also stem from our own perception of the relationship between what we consider as work and reward. One of the problems is we have got used to measuring one's success by the value of their possessions rather than the quality of their life.

At the end of the day, good quality of life is what most of us strive to achieve. Achieving true work-life balance is not necessarily in correlation to the number of days we work.

For the last five and a half years, finding ways to balance work and life has been my mission. My goal has been to build a life I don't need to take a vacation from. My thoughts have been that since we have such an advancement in technology, why are we still having to work 35-40 hours a week?

Technologies brought us time-saving devices to our domestic life, and we have embraced this.

Media have been reporting that AI is going to take our jobs away as if it was a threat to our working life. However, I have been personally looking forward to that day when AI takes over our mundane part of our job. I personally welcome the time when accountants no longer have to sit in front of a computer churning numbers or processing paperwork.

During my time as a finance professional in a corporate environment, because of the nature of our work, as for most accounting professionals, I was unable to take time off at the beginning and the end of each month, because of the accounting cycles. I definitely could not take any time off at financial year-end in preparation to audit and budget which usually clashed with school's Easter holiday break.

For this reason, rather than four days a week arrangement, flexibility in how and where I worked would have been more helpful to balance work and life. My request for this sort of flexibility was turned down at the time.

Had I requested a four-day arrangement and if accepted, I would have lost 20% of my earnings because the industry measures one's earnings by the number of hours worked. At that time, I thought I needed every penny I was earning as a single parent with a large mortgage.

Feeling unhappy and exhausted, I wanted to explore an idea of being paid for completing job tasks thinking if I could complete all the work within 4 days each week, I should not have to sacrifice my income.

Basically, promoting the idea of 'pay per productivity'.

Jobs like accounting is a lot easier to measure because there are a set of deadlines to meet each month and tasks to complete. I looked for a company and organisations that pay their staff by productivity rather than how many hours they worked. But unfortunately, the majority of the corporate environment does not seem to work that way… yet.

However, at the time of writing, I have heard that a few British firms have begun a four day a week arrangement for their employees with full pay. This is following a successful trial in New Zealand where they found that employees productivity increased by 20% by changing from five days a week to four days a week. Isn't that interesting?

Smart Zen for Organisations.

When you become aware of how much your connection and alignment to the universal force affects your overall health, well-being and happiness, you cannot help but look at areas of your life beyond your immediate set of family, home and friends.

If you are working in an organisation, or have people working with you or for you in your own business or organisation you run yourself, you are creating a micro-environment in itself.

People you work with; perhaps your colleagues or the staff you employ, but whatever the status or the position they hold, they hold influence over your mental status in the same way that you have an influence over theirs.

Just like in any other human to human relationship, the dynamics of it are greatly influenced by the contributions of each person as a member of that relationship. That contribution may be a positive force where it ignites the member's passion and enthusiasm, to promote growth, love, compassion, joy and respect.

The contribution can also have the opposite effect in that it causes negative and harmful energy affecting members to be de-motivated and to develop resentment and blame. That type of contribution can spiral downwards quickly affecting the whole organisation and cause increased stress and tension.

I am aware that not everyone wants to own their own business or become an entrepreneur. Some people prefer to work a set of hours where their responsibilities are clear, and they can go home and switch off. They also prefer to have a salary each month, which can make life easier to plan for personal finance.

When people contemplate leaving their job either for another or to set up their own business, the majority of times it is because they are not happy where they are.

Sometimes, they might even enjoy the job itself but cannot get on with their colleagues or their boss.

If you have employees, they may not feel as passionate about your business like you; to them, the success of your business is not at the top of their priority list. They have their own interests to look after and it may not be anything to do with your business or your life.

But that is okay.

As long as you are heading toward the same direction of growth, wealth, health and happiness and contributions to the wider world.

Like any relationship, it is a lot easier to work with people who have the same values and purpose in general. We have been discussing how stress can cause physical and mental health issues, it is important to make sure you are working with people who do not contribute to negativity.

The atmosphere depends on the energy of people who fill it.

The usual way of recruiting someone is through interviews

and CVs discussing their experiences and skills. Employers evaluate candidates based on how well they fit with the role through a series of questioning. It is very common for them to look for attributes like team worker, self-initiative and organisation skills. While those attributed have their own place in the selection process, what is sometimes missed is how well the candidate's deeper personal purpose fits into the overall dynamic of the organisation.

Organisations work best when everyone in it can work in a harmonious way just like a music band, orchestra or a pair of ice dancers. They exchange invisible energy as they perform tasks and in doing so you can create either the dynamics of great achievements or a potion mix of poisonous energy.

In the selection process, it is unquestionably important to discuss their dreams, aspirations and desires from both sides. You want people to come and work for you not just because of the money you are going to pay but because it is spiritually beneficial for both sides. You want someone to come and bring more energy into the area of the workplace where something was missing. You also want to be an employer who can provide an opportunity for your employee's personal growth, great job satisfaction and rewards for their contribution.

"Train people well enough so they can leave, treat them well enough so they don't want to."

- Richard Branson

In Japan, it had been the norm for people to join a company as a graduate and work for them all their life until retirement. Companies expected them to be that faithful and in return, they rewarded them by moving their ranks by age, not necessarily by their skills or performance. Moving jobs used to be frowned upon and gave you a big disadvantage, and in doing so, you would often end up working under someone younger than you.

Nowadays, young people move jobs on average every two years in the UK. The majority are more mobile and adaptable. Rather than being stuck in the same job, they aspire to expose themselves to different organisations and gain new experience.

As an employer, you have to learn to expect that your staff will not stay forever unless the relationship fulfils a lot of important elements. Likewise, you don't want your staff to stay unless they are happy because unhappy staff can be a great burden to your organisation financially and spiritually.

Is it Netflix that offer to pay some money for employees to leave if they are unhappy in an attempt to keep the workplace a harmonious, positive, engaged and productive environment?

I have met and still know many people who are very unhappy in their job but are not doing anything about changing that situation. Sometimes because they lack confidence in finding another job. Other times they blame their unhappiness on to their employer who they believe is supposed to fix it for them. So, they wait, well, sometimes forever because they are unable to take responsibility for their own destiny.

Provided that you find a suitable candidate and you are excited to work together. But as soon as you hire them you should also be preparing for their time to leave. Your job as an employer is to be a good leader for them so that they can grow spiritually as a person as well as providing opportunities for them to unleash their full potential.

Instead of trying to hold on to good staff by creating an environment where they feel powerless to be in control of their life, you would rather they feel it is a great place to work and they want to stay because your presence, your attitude, your vision and leadership energises them, inspire them and therefore they feel they want to contribute more.

How many employers are actually doing that?

It is often said that good staff are hard to retain. I personally say that is because good leaders and harmonious work environment are hard to find.

Employers often make a mistake of trying to retain staff by offering benefits like more pay, free gym membership or a company car. But they are missing the point. Those benefits are not unique. They can get the same things by working for others.

People are generally looking for something deeper than that. Many employers are not receptive to this or don't know how to deal with an unhappy workforce. Job satisfaction or loyalty cannot be bought by offering private medical scheme or throwing lavish Christmas parties for staff. They cannot necessarily be motivated by a company's Powerpoint presentation of visions and three-year plans.

Goal Setting for SmartZen Organisations

I think it is time that organisations start using a new acronym for goal setting called SMARTZEN instead of the traditional SMART goal.

This is how it goes;

S – Sustainable – the products and services the business sells and provide are from sustainable sources from sourcing materials, manufacturing method to packaging.

M – Motivational – the business promotes positive energy to customers, its employees and associates of the organisation. It works to collaborate rather than to compete in the market.

A - Agile – the business has an ability to adapt to change in environmental needs, technological advancement and innovations.

R - Responsible – the business operates with social and corporate responsibility in all areas from banking to logistics.

T- Transforming – the products and services are truly transforming rather than to create more clutter or excess in people's lives.

Z- Zen -the products and services promote harmony, balance and peace in the universe.

E – Ecological – the operation is managed with a conscience to the earth's ecology and how it affects the dynamics of all concerned.

N – Notable – the business is proud to be known for its positive contribution to the world, and actively speak out for the value it provides rather than the profit it achieves.

I hear the words of John Lennon and Yoko Ono Lennon as I write this.

"You may say, I am a dreamer, but I'm not the only one. I hope someday you will join us, and the world will live as one".

I really hope so.

HOW YOU GIVE

"If you want happiness for a year, inherit a fortune. If you want happiness for a lifetime, help someone else".

- Confucius

It seems nowadays everyone can say they are a life coach and everyone else seems to be in need of a life coach. Of course, the reasons for hiring a coach or consultant vary from taking action on something specific to accomplishing a big goal. So, will your life coach or lifestyle consultant actually help change your life?

Your Higher Needs

As I have been saying; more than any other time in history, we are living in a world where we have an abundance of food, material goods, and breakthrough advancements in health care and technology.

We have all the information at our fingertips, more knowledge and a better understanding of one's mind than ever before. In other words, in developed countries, people have never had it this good.

We have literally reached the top level of Maslow's hierarchy of needs. We have accomplished and have the prior basic and psychological needs met.

So why do people hire a coach or consultant to help change their life? Does anyone need to change their life anyway?

To understand this and where we are at, it is useful to refer to Maslow's theory.

Let's take a look at us and how we live. We have shelter in which we call home where we can feel safe. We have means of paying for our food, access to decent health care and policing that keeps us safe and well.

We live in a society where we are encouraged to belong to networks of communities and social circles where we feel a sense of belonging from a very early age. This could be school, university or workplace as well as local community and clubs. The Internet has made it even easier to connect with people all over the world.

Having met those needs, the next level of our need is self-esteem, according to Maslow. This need actually has been met for us for many years if you live in a developed country. We have created a system whereby everyone can receive education for free for at least 12 years of their life. Through education, we develop knowledge in packaged form in a relatively short time. The essential and vital knowledge which our human ancestors took years, sometimes centuries to research, find and collate through trial, error and indeed sweat and blood are available for us.

You don't have to walk around the earth to discover, first

that it is in a shape of a sphere and where you are on the earth in terms of location in relation to rest of the world or even in relation to the rest of the solar system and the galaxy. We also know that we are standing on this earth simply because of the earth's gravity and that it is not the sun that is rises and sets but the earth is spinning on its own axis. The knowledge we take for granted today have been given to us, all thanks to those clever people who found out these facts and shared it with us.

Through education and its institutions, we learn how we make a contribution to our society as an individual and in return develop a sense of self-worth and value. As children grow up into adulthood, the majority take with them the sense they are worthy of achievements, recognition and respect from others.

Such development and self-esteem give people the confidence to follow their aspirations and achieve their goals to receive further recognitions such as accolade, qualifications and then onto a career of their choice.

So, most people who seek life coaching or advice from consultants are at the stage where they have accomplished the prior levels and met those needs but not feeling quite happy or fulfilled.

They might be earning or belong to a household which generates higher income than the average which is about £28,000 in the UK for example.

They might be maintaining a reasonable lifestyle of having some disposable income to spend on luxuries such as eating out in restaurants or occasional long-haul holidays. They might hold a responsible job in a company where they feel respected and maintain a sense of belonging.

The majority of people seeking high-level support from a coach or a consultant fit into this category.

But somehow, they have come to a crossroad in life where they feel something is still missing.

Sometimes this could be because they are in a job, they no longer feel passionate about or the job or the company is not aligned with their belief or ethos.

It may be that their personal life is at crossroads or having to re-evaluate their important relationship.

For others, this could be because they are the age of reflection. Usually around 40 to 50 years of age, people start being aware of their own mortality. They start asking themselves questions like, 'Is there more to life than this?'

Coming to a realisation that you may not have been leading a life you wanted in your heart, accompanied by a sudden feeling that you are getting old might come as a shock.

This often accompanies the feeling they have not yet been able to accomplish what they believe they are truly capable of.

In other words, they feel they have not yet reached their full potential.

Whether you then curl up in the foetal position in despair of how much time you have wasted or view this as an opportunity for change depends on your outlook on life.

You might call this a wake-up call and take it as a chance to radically transform your life. This might mean discovering ways for you to unleash your full potential with the help of a life coach or a lifestyle consultant.

You might have noticed that throughout this book I have been taking you on the journey of fulfilling each stage of

Maslow's hierarchy of needs from Physiological, Safety, Love and how you relate to others, Self Esteem through personal development, Self-actualisation through recognising the impact you have on the wider world.

Transcendent Level

If you have already taken the leap in transforming your life by reviewing your goals, aspirations and taking action towards achieving them, you have probably accomplished a level of success and the social status already.

Perhaps you had a necessary drive in yourself without having your life coach help change your life.

Having accomplished some of your goals, if you are feeling something is still missing, this might be because you feel the purpose of your existence is not yet fulfilled.

Life is a bit like that.

We are here to continually grow and for people who have a mission to fulfil, there is no time to sit back and enjoy the retirement.

Some of the most inspirational people never retire from the work they have passion for.

Take Sir David Attenborough as an example, at the age of 92, he still works alongside the productions of nature documentary series and he launched a campaign on Climate Change at United Nation's Summit in 2018.

You might also be feeling you have something more to give. You might be feeling that you want to impact the world beyond family and friends. You believe there is something more to life than having the freedom of income, to be a beach bum or just living a life of excess.

You have been hearing a calling that might be described as spiritual insight.

This is the highest level of human need that we eventually strive to meet. Whether you believe in reincarnation or not, you feel that you have a duty beyond your own ego. You might be wanting to help others beyond your family, friends or customers or improve a system. Perhaps this is for all humankind, other species on earth or the whole ecology we belong to.

This vision is probably bigger than you have ever imagined

and having accomplished some success you are ready to go higher and help make changes to the wider world.

This happens with the first understanding of our own self and the relationship with the rest of the universe. We must first become aware of our own existence in the cosmos.

Reaching the transcendence level is not simply about being altruistic. You do not reach this state simply by donating money to charity or doing charitable work. This is a holistic and spiritual level that transcends beyond the physical realm.

You could say this is the level you were meant to reach in order to leave behind a meaningful legacy for all. It could be that you feel, this level is where you as a person will truly flourish.

I recently watched a Japanese international rugby player, Nagare Yutaka being interviewed on TV and I was totally amazed at his comments. Most of the time I see sports person talk about winning the next match, competition or tournament being their goal. But not, Nagare. He said something in the line of 'to create rugby that people will want to come and watch and to create a longing amongst children and youngsters to take up the sport, I think is our mission'.

He said 'mission', as if this is a task he has been given to do by something greater than him. This is the way winners and world-changers think. They think beyond their own gain or what they want for themselves. To them, they see their life purpose as their duty to play at the transcendent level.

You too have been put on this earth for a purpose. So what do you think that purpose is? What could be your life's mission?

What is Ikigai?

This Japanese word has recently been discussed and explained in the West and I am a little surprised in a similar way that I am surprised that chicken katsu is now a commonly known Japanese dish among English people.

In some publications, it even claims to be the Japanese secret to a long and happy life.

Ikigai, with no direct translation in English, means somewhat similar to 'purpose in life' that I talked about in the previous pages. Ikigai is what gets you out of bed in the morning. When you have Ikigai, you have hope for the future and reasons to carry on.

When people don't have Ikigai, they often shrivel up and die.

If you have devoted your life to someone, something, and they have left you, you might have lost your Ikigai at the same time.

Then you have to find another Ikigai. Ikigai is the essence of our well-being.

What is your Ikigai?

Take a moment to think about this.

Accepting the Middle Way

Earlier on I talked about developing self-awareness from early years and how encouraging collective interest is different from abnegation of self.

Some of us may have grown up believing albeit subconsciously, self-meekness and self-sacrifice is good and necessary. Often this leads to subconscious self-flagellation of our physical and emotional status whenever we desire something better for ourselves. We easily mistake it as being kind and thoughtful. And after many years of being in a marriage, relationship or raising children, where we exercised this sacrifice, we might find that no one is grateful for it after all.

Then as if some kind of explosion has taken its place in our mind, we experience what we sometimes call 'the middle life crisis'. We may decide to file for a divorce or feel a sudden need to quit the job, spend lots of money on something elaborate or sell everything and move into a commune where you try to generate your own electricity.

…but all such an extreme step.

In Zen Buddhism, we talk about accepting the middle way.

The middle way is between being extremely selfish and being extremely self-denial.

As I mentioned that I had been torn between wanting to create wealth and wanting to be spiritually enlightened.

If you also suffer from these two seemingly opposite statuses, it could be where you have created a block within yourself from achieving what you desire.

But again, harmony could be found there.

As mentioned earlier, in pursuit of happiness, we have to accept mistakes, defeats, failures, obstacles, all the negative emotions such as anger; sadness, frustration, jealousy, selfishness and procrastination as part of life. We cannot truly experience happiness without also experiencing the opposite.

This does not mean we have to dwell in the negative. It does not mean, you need to go about your days, thinking about all the bad things that have happened to you or are happening now.

If you are suffering from the effects of failures or obstacles seemingly in your way, is it because you believe that life should not be this way?

If you think life should be easy and ALWAYS happy, then sure you are in this life for a disappointment. If you were brought up in a family who made you believe that life is good and there is no evil. It would come as a surprise that the world is full of EVIL.

But if instead, you go about it in your daily life believing that life is meant to be full of challenges and obstacles in the first place, the fact that life is full of those is no longer a problem.

Because when good comes your way, you have a greater appreciation for it.

I came across this idea in the West when I read a book called Road Less Travelled by Dr Scott Peck.

This is also part of the teaching of Buddhism.

The acceptance that life is difficult is not the same as treating life as a compromise. There is a big difference in viewing life as a compromise and taking the middle path.

The simple fact is that just like the symbol of yin and yang, the universe is made up of two opposing elements, light and dark and good and evil, etc. as they co-exist with one another.

Acceptance is about recognising the existence of two sides as part of the whole.

Within us, there are also two sides. Although we are complex being, we tend to make a judgement albeit subconsciously, about whether something is good or bad.

When something bad happens, we judge it as negative without seeing the opposite meaning and learn something from it.

Take a simple thing like weather, it constantly changes, especially if you live in the UK. If it rains, is it good weather or bad weather?

If you had expected a sunny dry day for your garden barbeque and it pours, you might consider the rain to be bad. But after a dry spell, you wanted a rainy day so your garden plants could be replenished with water, the rain is a welcome gift to the starving roses and lavenders in your garden.

If someone is mean to you, it is easy to think that that person is in the wrong, they are placed in the list of terrible people you know in your book. But at the same time, you know that there is something positive about that person and an element you can admire. An angle you can respect.

Or it might give you an opportunity for you to appreciate more all the other lovely people around you that help make your life a joy to live.

When you learn to see each situation from another angle or to change your perspective, you dis-engage from your own limiting belief.

In a way, we cannot control the weather, but the thought is something we can control. There is no need to place anything on one side or the other of good and evil. There is no need to categorise or judge anything into one section of your mid or another.

Acceptance is knowing that there are two sides to every coin.

That includes you.

For example, you can be productive and also be lazy. You can be kind and also be spiteful. You can be generous and you can be tight. You can be happy and also be depressed. You can be light and you can also be dark.

As soon as you can accept both sides, neither side can threaten you any longer. When you know that you can be a complete bitch, you can choose not to be.

That is the power of acceptance.

Denying one side of you keeps you within your own limitations. If you cannot accept that there is a part of you that can be horrible, you are a danger to society as well as to yourself.

Many of us know this subconsciously, if we don't, we cannot have created a relatively safe social environment where people can work and live side by side peacefully.

We know that anyone has the ability to be aggressive if necessary, including ourselves, but we choose not to because we feel at peace with our own negative side.

Being at peace with oneself comes from accepting yourself as a whole and therefore being in a place to be able to accept others.

Now you might make a mistake of thinking that taking the middle way is like being neither here or there. Or being vague in your existence or not having a strong stance on something. You might even consider being in the middle is being unremarkable, plain or damn right boring.

But take a look around you. Taking the middle way is where many wise and successful people walk.

The greatest people in our history who left us the legacy of peace and happiness were all promoter of this middle way, harmony and the right balance.

Dr Martin Luther King's vision was not to get rid of the whites, he called for harmony between the white and the black.

John Lennon and Yoko Ono, their relentless work and campaigns for peace speak to you of the interconnected world we can share, not an exclusion.

Nelson Mandela's vision was for democracy and equality rather than the constraints of white man's views of how the world should be.

What can you give to this world through the understanding of accepting the existence of both side of the coin?

Without denying the opposite how could you help spread an abundance of love, peace and wealth to the rest of the world?

How could you fulfil your own purpose in life and your desire to flourish, and simultaneously work towards collective interest?

What will be the biggest contribution to the future generations that you can leave behind? How will people remember you for?

Someone who had 10 sports cars in a garage? Or someone who opened 10 schools in deprived areas?

A multi-millionaire who travelled in a private jet? Or a multi-millionaire who made a difference to the people and places he travelled to?

How about... being one of the most famous people in history who made a fortune through social media? Or the most famous person in history who changed the fortune of the natural world, its ecology and therefore the planet?

What will the world expect from you in your lifetime? What part of yourself can you give to the world to make it a better place? Your knowledge, skills, inspiration, your influence, love and vision?

Every one of us is part of the whole.

Develop more compassion for the universal network you

belong to. You are part of the larger interconnected network and what you do makes a difference and affects all.

The Balancing Act

I have covered many topics in this book. If you are new to the idea of harmony, balance and inner peace, the SmartZen concept may take a while to sink in.

As a foundation, I hope you can see that we live in the interconnected network of ecology, society, community and friends and family. You also live in a body which is also an interconnected network of physical cells, molecules, energy in body, mind and spirit.

The harmony within those networks is the optimal status. The status we sometimes call, being in the zone, being at optimal performance, experiencing synchronicity or being in tune.

That is exactly the reason that the work has to start from within you and before you can work to help others and change the world.

When that harmony becomes the default status, a passion,

a mission, a purpose or Ikigai emerges that is truly authentic to you, uninfluenced by anything else.

But you also know that in order to satisfy your passion, to complete your mission, to achieve your purpose or to maintain your Ikigai, the only way is to not break that harmony.

Because it is now logical that the right balance is best maintained in order that happiness, success, wealth and health can be manifested as a result.

Happiness is a state of being that you can 'already' find within you.

Success follows happiness and by taking the middle way you lead your life based on how much difference you make in people's lives, the natural world and the planet we live on.

Finally...

I hope you have enjoyed this book and found out how some Japanese wisdom can be adapted positively to our present lives.

I also hope you use this as a useful guide to transforming your life into a more balanced and abundant life full of wealth, good health and happiness.

But it needs to be reminded that the journey of transformation, spiritual awakening or balanced state is not a fixed destination.

The way or the path is a never-ending journey and you need to keep travelling. Just like the seasons, the scenery keeps changing. Some part of us die and another part of us renewed.

That is the nature of things.

The SmartZen Programs

SmartZen is a way of life. As a SmartZen lifestyle consultant, my job is to take you from where you are to where you want to be in life so that you unleash your full potential, flourish fully and attain what you desire through a holistic and balanced approach.

One on One SmartZen Program

I work with professionals and entrepreneurs who have attained a certain level of success but feeling stuck, burned out, stressed or simply bored. I help them find their happiness, balance and inner peace leading to discovering their life's mission and help achieve a new level of success.

Email me your best number to yumi@smartzen.org to book a free consultation and discover how SmartZen method can help you transform your life.

Online Resources and Events

To discover our next events and valuable tips and information, please visit www.smartzen.org

A Note from Yumi

Although I was brought up by Japanese parents who tied to instil Japanese traditional values in me, I rebelled against and broke away from their idea of conformity, discipline and groupism in my teens.

In my early 20s, I had an opportunity to explore the inner workings of my mind through a psychoanalytic therapy which had a profound impact on me. Through the understanding of my childhood and how much my experience and conditioning were affecting me as I was entering adulthood, my perspectives on 'life' changed completely as I entered the world of introspection.

As I grew older, I became aware of part of Japanese culture that I respect, resonate and agree and other parts of the culture that I dislike, condemn, feel ashamed of as my root. Equally, there is part of the Western culture I love and respect as well as some parts which I find disappointing since I have lived in the UK for over 30 years.

I hope we can pick the good bits of both cultures and create a common theme with ideas which are no longer foreign to any of us.

A path of self-discovery with the help of a good coach/counsellor/consultant works very well to transform lives and help unleash one's true potential.

I hope you explore an opportunity to transform yours.

About the Author

Yumi is a certified life coach, a Reiki master and a business consultant.

She works with individuals to help redesign their life to lead a life of true happiness and prosperity. She also works with organisations to help implement effective methods to increase productivity and to enhance the work-life balance of their workforce.

From dual perspectives of Japanese culture and British culture, she teaches you to adopt simple ideas derived from Japanese Zen philosophy to stay true to your happiness and inner harmony while pursuing success.

As a result, the transformation you experience will be holistic and eternal.

References and Credits

*1 YouGov plc 2015, cited Coleman Alison 2015 'Over half of UK workers have experienced 'burnout' in their job' (online) available at https://www.virgin.com/disruptors/over-half-uk-workers-have-experienced-burnout-their-job

*2 The 2015 Workplace Flexibility Study, 'Survey Finds Disconnect Between Employers and Employees On Work-Life Balance' (online) available at https://workplacetrends.com/the-2015-workplace-flexibility-study/

*3 Health and Safety Executive (HSE) cited Sarner Moya 2018, 'How Burnout Became a Sinister and Insidious Epidemic' (online) available at https://www.theguardian.com/society/2018/feb/21/how-burnout-became-a-sinister-and-insidious-epidemic

*4-Lebowitz Shana and Akhtar Allana 2019, '14 Rich and Powerful People Share Their Surprising Definition of Success' (online) available at https://www.businessinsider.com/how-successful-people-define-success-2017-3?r=UK&IR=T

*5- 'Mental Health Statistics: Stress, Results of the Mental Health Foundation's Study 2018' (online) available at https://www.mentalhealth.org.uk/statistics/mental-health-statistics-stress

*6- Thomson Scott, 'The Advantages of Meditative Space in the Workplace' (online) available at https://work.chron.com/advantages-meditative-space-workplace-1085.html
Garvey Marianne 2018, 'Meditation Rooms Are the Hottest New Work Perk' (online) available at https://www.marketwatch.com/story/meditation-rooms-are-the-hottest-new-work-perk-2018-10-26
McKay Sarah 2016, 'The Neuroscience of Mindfulness Meditation' (online) available at https://chopra.com/articles/the-neuroscience-of-mindfulness-meditation?_ga=2.70403152.176325902.1549299912-274211348.1549299912